Outstanding Dissertations in **Linguistics**

General Editor
Jorge Hankamer
University of California, Santa Cruz

A Garland Series

Operations on Lexical Forms

Unaccusative Rules in Germanic Languages

Lori S. Levin

Garland Publishing, Inc. ■ New York & London
1988

Copyright © 1988 Lori S. Levin
All Rights Reserved

Library of Congress Cataloging-in-Publication Data

Levin, Lori.
Operations on lexical forms : unaccusative rules in Germanic
languages / Lori S. Levin.
p. cm. — (Outstanding dissertations in linguistics) Originally
presented as the author's thesis (Ph.D. —Massachusetts Institute of
Technology, 1986)
Bibliography: p.
ISBN 0-8240-5190-4
1. Lexical-functional grammar. 2. English language—Grammar,
Generative. 3. Dutch language—Grammar, Generative. I. Title.
II. Series.
P158.25.L48 1988
430—dc19   88-16585

Printed on acid-free, 250-year-life paper
Manufactured in the United States of America

PREFACE

I had to re-read this thesis in order to prepare it for publication and found that I had forgotten how much some of the ideas have evolved since the time the thesis was written. In fact, I found that, when I wrote the thesis, I was struggling to write down ideas that were not completely formed, so I am glad to be have the chance to write a preface which puts everything in perspective.

The most important contribution of this thesis is a representation of unaccusativity in Lexical Functional Grammar. When I first started to work on this problem, the challenge was to account for a phenomenon which seemed to require a deep or initial level of representation in a theory of syntax that does not have a deep or initial level of representation. (Since constituent structure in LFG represents the surface word order and constituency of a sentence and functional structure represents its *surface* grammatical relations, there is no way of showing that subjects of some verbs are deep or initial objects.) Furthermore, there was a challenge in accounting for unaccusativity in a way that was in the spirit of LFG without sneaking in a level of deep structure or compromising the fundamental principles of LFG.

The account of unaccusativity that I came up with is tied to a theory of relation changing rules as linking rules. In this theory, relation changes such as passivization and dative shift are the result of alternate linkings of grammatical functions to thematic roles. For example, the agent role can link to the subject function and the theme role to the object function or the agent role can link to an oblique function while the theme role links to the subject function. Thus related forms of the same verb are not derived from one basic form but are derived in parallel by different linking rules.

In order to represent unaccusativity in a linking theory, I introduced a two-step linking process. First, thematic roles are linked to something called Argument Classification, which distinguishes between unaccusative and unergative verbs. Then argument classification is linked to grammatical functions. Chapter 2 describes some properties of relation changing rules (including unaccusativity) that this two-step linking process accounts for; Chapter 3 describes the two-step liking theory; and Chapters 4 and 5 formulate relation changing rules in English and Dutch using this theory.

This new approach to relation changing rules constitutes a valuable contribution to LFG because, in addition to allowing for the formulation of rules that apply to unaccusative verbs, it captures the similarity of unaccusative verbs and passive verbs; provides explanations for a number of fundamental properties of relation changing rules (Chapter 2); and include principles which make predictions about possible and impossible relation changing rules. Furthermore, the theory is different from other syntactic theories in that all relation changing rules are lexical and that grammatical functions are not defined in terms of phrase structure or thematic roles. And, although Argument Classification looks at first like a level of representation analogous to deep structure, it is different in a way that leads to interesting analyses of double object constructions and certain unpassivizable predicates (Section 4.2).

Two other important contributions in this thesis are the discussion of non-nominative subjects and the discussion of unaccusative mismatches. Non-nominative subjects pose a problem for LFG in two ways. First, they are connected to the issue of unaccusativity in that verbs with non-nominative subjects are unaccusative in many languages. Second, non-nominative subjects exhibit mixed subjecthood behavior; that is, they behave like subjects in some ways but not others and this has been taken as evidence for an inversion rule which introduces multiple derivational layers of grammatical relations (Perlmutter 1979, 1982). (Hermon's (1981) analysis of non-nominative subjects in Government and Binding theory also uses multiple levels of representation.) In Chapter 4, I show that, not only can LFG handle certain kinds of mixed subjecthood behavior, but it actually predicts which patterns of mixed subjecthood behavior will occur.[1]

Unaccusative mismatches arise when one rule (such as passivization) treats a verb as unaccusative while another rule (such as auxiliary selection) treats it as unergative. This is unexpected for a syntactic representation of unaccusativity because a verb cannot be both unaccusative and unergative at the same time, and the conflicts cannot be resolved by giving these verbs two entries, one unaccusative and one unergative. Because of observations such as these, some linguists have begun to question the syntactic basis of unaccusativity and look more toward lexical semantics for explanations of unaccusative phenomena. (See Van Valin

---

[1] In Chapter 5 I show that the same predictions hold in Dutch. However, Zaenen ("The Place of *bevallen* (please) in the Syntax of Dutch," ms. Xerox PARC and CSLI), taking additional data into account, shows that the situation is more complex and presents a rather different analysis tied in with a theory of word order as well as a theory of linking.

(1987)[2] and Zaenen (1987).[3]) In this thesis and in later work (L. Levin 1987[4]), I maintain that, although unaccusativity has a lexical semantic basis, it is still necessary to have a syntactic projection of unaccusativity so that syntactic rules can identify unaccusative verbs. The mismatches are resolved here by proposing that the syntactic representation of unaccusativity is necessary but not sufficient for some rules and that the formulation of these rules includes further semantic restrictions.

The theory of relation changing rules with argument classification has continued to develop since the completion of this thesis and a number of issues are now treated differently. I will mention three such issues here: the status of OBJ2, the lexical encoding of transitivity, and the exact nature of argument classification.

L. Levin (1987) and Bresnan (1987)[5] now treat OBJ2 as a semantically restricted function like the oblique functions instead of as a semantically unrestricted function like SUBJ and OBJ. Since the distinction between semantically restricted and unrestricted functions is central in the theory as the basis of argument classification (Chapter 3), the change in status of OBJ2 leads to major changes in the analysis of double object constructions (Section 4.2).

The issue surrounding transitivity in LFG with argument classification is whether verbs have to be explicitly subcategorized for an OBJ function or whether the presence of OBJ in a lexical form is predictable from rules that link thematic roles to grammatical functions. In this thesis, I take the view that transitivity has to be explicitly represented for each verb because non-thematic objects for verbs like *believe* are not predictable and could not otherwise be generated. However, in L. Levin (1987), I propose a different account of non-thematic objects which removes the need for explicit subcategorization for OBJ.

The most important development in the theory since the writing of this thesis is a change in the nature of argument classification, which resulted from discussions with Joan Bresnan, K.P. Mohanan, and Annie Zaenen at the Center for the Study of Language and Information in 1987. Now, argument classifications are seen simply as underspecified

---

[2] R.D. Van Valin, Jr., "The Unaccusative Hypothesis vs Lexical Semantics: Syntactic vs Semantic Approaches to Verb Classification," *Proceedings of NELS 17*.

[3] A. Zaenen, "Are there Unaccusative Verbs in Dutch?" *Proceedings of NELS 17*.

[4] L. Levin, "Toward a Linking Theory of Relation Changing Rules in LFG," to appear as a CSLI Technical Report, Center for the Study of Language and Information, Stanford University.

[5] J. Bresnan, "On Locative Inversion in Chichewa," *CSLI Monthly*, vol. 2, no. 8.

grammatical functions which are associated with thematic roles by linking rules. These underspecified grammatical functions are then fully specified by default rules or by marked linking specifications. Subjects of unaccusative verbs and passive verbs are underspecified in a way that allows them to surface as subjects or objects whereas subjects of transitive verbs and unergative verbs are underspecified in a way that allows them to link to subject (in active sentences) or to oblique (in passive sentences), but not to object.

The main difference between argument classification and the newer view of underspecified linkings is that the new view does not use argument classification as an explicit level of representation. Nevertheless, it is still possible to account for many unaccusative phenomena. Bresnan (1987) and Bresnan and Kanerva (in preparation)[6] use underspecified linkings in the formulation of passivization and locative inversion in Chichewa and show how locative inversion can apply to unaccusative and passive verbs without applying to unergative and active transitive verbs. L. Levin (1987) presents revised analyses of passivization, control, and the English pleonastic *there* construction. The use of underspecified grammatical functions in linking rules seems promising because it leads to treatments of relation changing rules which are not only elegant, but interesting because of the new insights that they provide.

L. Levin
Pittsburgh, PA
November, 1987

---

[6] J. Bresnan and J. Kanerva, "Locative Inversion in Chichewa." Stanford University.

Acknowledgements

I started writing this thesis while I was a graduate student at M.I.T. and finished it while teaching at the University of Pittsburgh. As a result, I have many people to thank and I ask everyone to understand that the brevity of these acknowledgements does not indicate lack of gratitude.

First, I thank my thesis advisor, Joan Bresnan, for her support, encouragement, and inspiration. I also thank my other committee members, Ken Hale, Haj Ross, and especially Annie Zaenen, who has been cheering me on ever since she advised me as an undergraduate at the University of Pennsylvania. I first started planning this thesis during the summer of 1982 while I was working as a summer student at Xerox PARC and I thank Ron Kaplan for making that possible and for helping me learn many details about LFG. Joan Maling also was a great help in the early stages when I thought that this thesis was going to be mostly about Icelandic.

I wish I could thank everyone at M.I.T. who took time to discuss my thesis, but I probably couldn't list all of them, so I'll just mention some very special people: Jane Simpson, Beth Levin, Malka Rappaport, Susan Rothestein, and Alec Marantz. I also thank Steve Bagley and my housemates at 15 Lawrence St. for making the whole thing more bearable and Brownell Chalstrom for always being very proud of me.

Some of the senior faculty in the Linguistics Department at Pitt have been very helpful and understanding even though I kept them on edge for two years. Thank-you, Christina Paulston, Sally Thomason, and especially Rich Thomason. Thanks also to Lori Taft, Laura Knecht, Judy Vernick, and Glynda Hull. I also thank all the students whose long papers and theses I am advising or have advised. I've learned a lot from them about writing a thesis.

I have a lot of friends in Pittsburgh whose support has made all the difference in the world. They include Billy Weil, Jeff Bonar, Kate McEvoy, and especially Jeff Shrager, who, for many years, has always been there when I needed a friend. I also thank my parents, Herman and Pauline Levin, who I think I have made very happy by finishing this. And I thank Paul O'Hanlon, who made a big difference in a short time.

On the more practical side of things, I thank my proof readers (Peggy Andersen, David McDermot, Faye Orlove, and Teruko Watanabe), my Dutch informants (especially Yolande Post), and Mike Kazar, who defined the Scribe environment for my example sentences.

Table of Contents

1. Introduction: Grammatical Relations and Relation Changing Rules — 10
    1.1. Grammatical Relations in LFG — 10
    1.2. The Role of Grammatical Relations in the Syntax of LFG — 12
    1.3. Relation Changes in LFG — 16
2. Some Properties of Relation Changing Rules — 22
    2.1. Semantic Conditioning of Relation Changing Rules — 22
    2.2. Syntactic Productivity of Relation Changing Rules — 30
    2.3. Unaccusative Rules — 36
        2.3.1. Resultative Secondary Predication. — 37
        2.3.2. The Pleonastic *there* Construction — 39
        2.3.3. Passivization in Dutch — 40
        2.3.4. Experiencer Inversion — 41
        2.3.5. Auxiliary Selection — 45
    2.4. SUBJs and OBJs — 51
3. A Theory of Relation Changing Rules — 53
    3.1. Semantically Restricted and Unrestricted Functions — 54
    3.2. Argument Classes — 57
    3.3. Another View of Argument Classes — 59
    3.4. Two Types of Relation Changing Rules — 61
        3.4.1. Classification of Thematic Arguments — 63
        3.4.2. Purely Syntactic Rules — 65
    3.5. Raising to Object and Transitivity — 69
    3.6. Properties of Relation Changing Rules — 73
4. Formulation of Rules: English — 75
    4.1. The Causative/Inchoative Rule — 76
        4.1.1. Formulation — 77
        4.1.2. The Causative/Inchoative Rule and Transitivity — 79
    4.2. Double Object Rules — 82
        4.2.1. The Representation of Double Object Constructions — 82
        4.2.2. Formulation of Double Object Rules — 86
        4.2.3. Comparison to Other Treatments of Double Object Constructions — 88
    4.3. Patient Rule — 91
    4.4. The Passive Rule — 92
        4.4.1. Formulation of the Rule — 92
        4.4.2. The Passive Rule and Transitivity — 93
        4.4.3. Advantages of a Subject Demotion Approach — 97
    4.5. Inversion Constructions in English — 100
        4.5.1. Formulation of English Inversion Rules — 101
        4.5.2. Subjecthood of Fronted PPs and Pleonastic *There* — 105

5. Formulation of Rules: Dutch — 110
5.1. Passivization — 110
5.1.1. Formulation of the Dutch Passive Rule — 110
5.1.2. The 1-Advancement Exclusiveness Law — 111
5.1.3. Syntactic and Semantic Properties of Unpassivizable Predicates — 112
5.2. Experiencer Inversion — 115
5.2.1. Formalization of Dutch Experiencer Inversion — 115
5.2.2. Subjecthood of the Nominative NP — 119
5.2.3. Objecthood of the Nominative NP — 121
5.2.4. Subjecthood of the Non-Nominative NP — 122
5.2.5. Objecthood of Non-Nominative NPs — 124
5.2.6. Conclusion — 125
5.3. Auxiliary selection and Rule Mismatches — 126
5.3.1. Description of Mismatches — 127
5.3.2. A Question about the Nature of Mismatches — 129
5.3.3. A Syntactic Account of Auxiliary Selection and Mismatches — 130
5.4. Conclusion — 132
6. REFERENCES — 133

Chapter 1
Introduction: Grammatical Relations and Relation Changing Rules

1.1. Grammatical Relations in LFG

Grammatical relations in LFG are represented in *lexical forms* which are part of the lexical entry of each verb. Lexical forms portray verbs as argument-taking predicates. Each form consists of a set of grammatical functions (GF) and a *predicate argument structure* (PAS) which lists the thematic roles of the verb's arguments. Each grammatical function is paired either with one of the verb's thematic role slots or with a non-thematic value such as a dummy element or a raised element from a lower clause. These assignments of grammatical functions to argument positions or to non-thematic values constitute *grammatical relations*.

(1) shows part of the lexical entry for the verb *kick*. Its pedicate argument structure contains the role names of its two thematic arguments (agent and patient) and is delimited by angle brackets. The grammatical function associated with each role is written directly below it. The symbols (↑ PRED) to the left of the equal sign tell us that this lexical form will appear as the value of a PRED feature in a functional structure.

(1)   (↑ PRED) = 'kick⟨ agent   patient ⟩'   *predicate argument structure*
                           SUBJ   OBJ   *grammatical functions*

Since grammatical relations match up grammatical functions with thematic roles, they play a role in the interpretation of sentences. For example, the lexical form for *kick* in (1) tells us that the subject of the verb *kick* is to be interpreted as its agent argument while the object is to be interpreted as its patient. This would be appropriate for an active sentence containing the verb *kick*, such as *Someone kicked the ball*.

The representation of grammatical relations can also indicate that some GFs are not interpreted as arguments of the verb. The lexical form for *seem* in (2) would be used in a sentence like *People seem to be happy*. It indicates that the XCOMP of *seem*, *to be happy*, plays the theme role and that the subject of *seem* is not a thematic argument of *seem*. Notice that the non-thematic SUBJ function is written outside of the angle brackets instead of being attached to a thematic role inside the brackets. The equation (↑ SUBJ) = (↑ XCOMP SUBJ) assigns a value to the SUBJ function. It says that the SUBJ of *seem* (*people* in this case) is also the SUBJ of the XCOMP *to be happy*. In short, (2) tells us that in *People seem to be happy*, the verb *seem* is a one place predicate and that its one argument is *to be happy* predicated of *people*.

(2)   (↑ PRED) = 'seem⟨ theme ⟩SUBJ'
                        XCOMP
       (↑ SUBJ) = (↑ XCOMP SUBJ)

In section 1.2 we will return to the role of grammatical relations in the interpretation of sentences. But first I will say more about the GFs and thematic role names which appear in lexical forms.

The GFs which can be used in lexical forms are SUBJ, OBJ, OBJ2, COMP, XCOMP, and the oblique functions (OBL_{agent}, OBL_{goal}, OBL_{source}, etc.) These are the *subcategorizable functions*. Other functions like MODIFIER, ADJUNCT, and FOCUS are not subcategorizable. They appear in functional structures but not in lexical forms.

In PASs I will use the role names agent, patient, source, goal, and theme in accordance with the definitions given in Hale and Laughren (1983). I will also use the role names experiencer and stimulus for experiencer verbs (e.g. *like, amuse, hate*). For verbs whose arguments do not have easily identifiable roles, like *honor*, I will use specific role names like honoror and honoree. The definitions which follow are adapted from Hale and Laughren.

Theme: something which is in some location or state, comes into or goes out of existence (at some location or state), or undergoes a change of location or state. The themes in (3) are italicized.

(3) a.   *The guests* arrived at the party.
    b.   *The butter* melted.
    c.   *A book* sat on the table.
    d.   He kicked *a hole* in the wall.
    e.   They started *the movie*.
    f.   *Nothing* happened.

Agent: an entity which produces an effect on some other entity, causes another entity to be in some location or state, causes another entity to come into/go out of existence, or causes another entity to undergo an change of location or state.

(4) a. *The wind* blew away the leaves.
    b. *The cook* melted the butter.
    c. *The projectionist* started the movie.
    d. *The player* kicked the ball.

Source: the starting point of a change of location or state or an entity which ceases to have possession of a theme.

(5) a. The kids walked *from home* to school.
    b. He changed *from a mild mannered reporter* into a heroic crime fighter.
    c. He bought a book *from her*.

Goal: the endpoint of a change of location or state, the place or state in which a theme comes into existence, or an entity which comes to have possession of a theme.

(6) a. They drove *to New York*.
    b. He poked a hole *in the wall*.
    c. He gave it *to them*.

Patient: a kind of goal. When an agent produces (i.e. brings into existence) an effect (theme) on an entity (goal), that entity is called a patient.

(7) a. The hunter shot *the bird*.
    b. The cook poked a hole in *the cake*.
    c. The cook poked *the cake* with a fork.
    d. The player kicked *the ball*.

1.2. The Role of Grammatical Relations in the Syntax of LFG

One requirement of an adequate theory of generative grammar is to map parts of sentences onto argument slots of verbs. For example, given a sentence like *Someone kicked the ball*, the rules of the grammar should associate *someone* with the agent role of *kick* and *the ball* with the patient role. In order to meet this requirement, LFG uses two submappings: function-structure association and function-argument association. Function-structure association assigns a grammatical function to each phrase in a sentence. In this example, *someone* gets the SUBJ function and *the ball* gets the OBJ function. Function-argument association assigns grammatical functions to thematic roles or to non-thematic values. In this case, the SUBJ function is associated with the agent role and the OBJ function is associated with the patient role.

Once we know that *someone* is the SUBJ of *kick* and that the SUBJ of *kick* is the agent of *kick*, we know that *someone* is the agent of *kick*. Similarly, once we know that *the ball* is the OBJ of *kick* and that the OBJ of *kick* is its patient, we know that *the ball* is the patient of *kick*. This constitutes understanding the sentence in the narrow sense of lexical semantics.

Function-structure association, also called syntactic encoding, takes place in the *constituent structure* (c-structure). C-structure is a language-particular representation of linear order, syntactic category, and constituency. It takes the familiar form of a phrase structure tree except that each node carries a set of annotations in addition to its label. The annotations identify, among other things, the grammatical function of each phrase. In the simplified c-structure (8), the equation (↑ SUBJ) = ↓ on the first NP means that the NP is the SUBJ of the sentence. The equation (↑ OBJ) = ↓ on the second NP identifies that NP as the OBJ. The equation ↑ = ↓ does not assign a grammatical function. Instead, it identifies heads of phrases and minor categories. The remaining equations in (8) contain information about the lexical items.

(8)

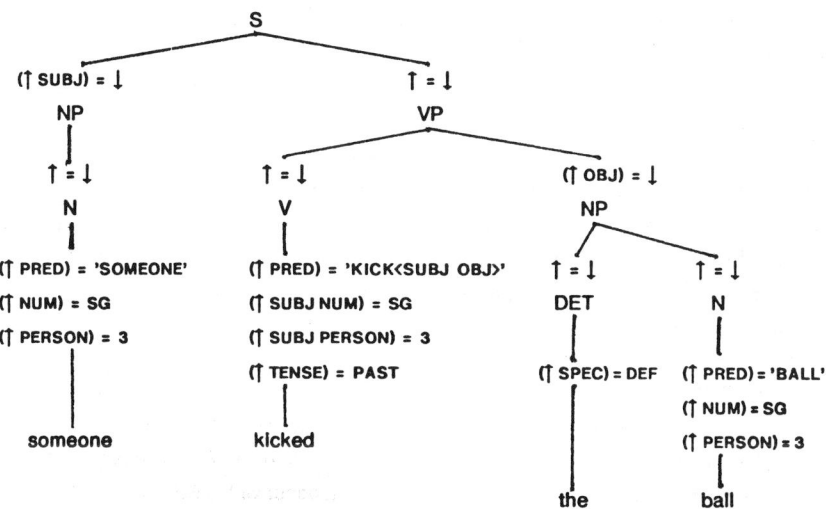

The equations which annotate the nodes are actually instructions for building *functional structures* (f-structures) where each phrase is represented as a set of features and values and is labelled by its grammatical function. The f-structure in (9) for *Someone kicked the ball* shows that *someone* is the SUBJ, *kick* is the PRED(icate), and *the ball* is the OBJ.

(9)
$$\begin{bmatrix} \text{SUBJ} & \begin{bmatrix} \text{PRED} & \text{'someone'} \\ \text{NUM} & \text{sg} \\ \text{PERSON} & 3 \end{bmatrix} \\ \text{PRED} & \text{'KICK< SUBJ OBJ >'} \\ \text{TENSE} & \text{past} \\ \text{OBJ} & \begin{bmatrix} \text{PRED} & \text{'ball'} \\ \text{NUM} & \text{sg} \\ \text{PERSON} & 3 \\ \text{SPEC} & \text{def} \end{bmatrix} \end{bmatrix}$$

C-structure represents word order and hierarchical structure, which may vary from language to language. However, in f-structure, linear order is irrelevant (the main components of (9) could have been ordered differently from top to bottom) and much of the language-particular constituent structure is flattened. As a result, there are many languages where the c-structure for *Someone kicked the ball* would look very different from the English c-structure but the f-structure would be basically the same except for values of some morphological features like TENSE and CASE.[6]

The annotated c-structure tree and the mapping from c-structure to f-structure associate phrases with grammatical functions. The other submapping, associating functions with thematic argument slots, takes place in lexical forms. The lexical form for *kick*, as explained earlier, says that the SUBJ is the agent and the OBJ is the patient. Functional structure therefore contains all the information necessary to associate phrases with thematic argument slots. It shows the grammatical functions of the phrases in the sentence and it shows the thematic roles of the functions.

In addition to representing grammatical relations, lexical forms also serve as subcategorization frames. In LFG, verbs are subcategorized for the grammatical functions they occur with, not for the structural context in which they appear. For example, the lexical form for *kick* in functional structure (9) says that *kick* must occur with a SUBJ and an OBJ.

---

[6] A language could have a different f-structure for *Someone kicked the ball* if the verb *kick* in that language assigned different grammatical functions to its agent and patient arguments. For example, in a truly ergative language, SUBJ might be assigned to the patient argument while OBJ is assigned to the agent argument (Marantz 1984, B. Levin 1983). In such a languge, the values of SUBJ and OBJ in f-structure would be reversed. There may also be languages where the patient of *kick* is oblique. In these languages, the function name OBL_{pat} would stand in place of OBJ in (9).

The conditions of Completeness and Coherence detect subcategorization violations *in functional structure*. An f-structure is *incomplete* if it does not contain all the grammatical functions listed in the verb's lexical form and an f-structure is *incoherent* if it contains subcategorizable functions that are not listed in the verb's lexical form.

More precisely, I assume that Completeness and Coherence are well-formedness conditions on clause nuclei. Clause nuclei are f-structures containing a lexical form and a SUBJ. (9) has three functional structures — the whole f-structure, the SUBJ, and the OBJ (each f-structure is surrounded by square brackets) — but of these, only the whole top-level f-structure is a clause nucleus.

(10) a. **Completeness:** A clause nucleus C containing a lexical form L is complete if every subcategorizable function name in L is locally contained in C.

b. **Coherence:** A clause nucleus C containing a lexical form L is coherent if every subcategorizable function locally contained in C is mentioned in L.

Complete and coherent f-structures correspond to grammatical sentences and genuine violations of Completeness and Coherence result in ungrammatical sentences, as f-structures ((11) a) and ((11) b) show. F-structure ((11) a) for the sentence *The baby slept cookies* is incoherent because the top-level clause nucleus contains an OBJ which is not mentioned in any lexical form. F-structure ((11) b) for the sentence *The cook omitted* is incomplete because the top-level clause nucleus does not contain the OBJ which is required by the lexical form for *omit*.

(11) a.

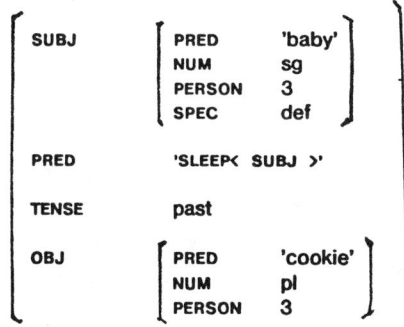

b.
$$\begin{bmatrix} \text{SUBJ} & \begin{bmatrix} \text{PRED} & \text{'cook'} \\ \text{NUM} & \text{sg} \\ \text{PERSON} & 3 \\ \text{SPEC} & \text{def} \end{bmatrix} \\ \text{PRED} & \text{'OMIT< SUBJ OBJ >'} \\ \text{TENSE} & \text{past} \end{bmatrix}$$

Notice that *The baby kicked* is grammatical in spite of the fact that lexical form (1) requires a SUBJ an an OBJ. This is because there is another lexical form for *kick* which requires only a SUBJ. This form is an alternative subcategorization frame for *kick* related to (1) by a lexical redundancy rule. Since there is well-formed f-structure for *The baby kicked* using (12) in place of (1), the grammar correctly represents the fact that the sentence is grammatical.

(12) (↑ PRED) = 'kick< agent   patient >'
                    SUBJ   ∅

This section has covered several points: grammatical relations, also called function-argument associations, are assignments of grammatical functions with thematic arguments or non-thematic values and they constitute half of a two-step mapping from phrases to argument slots; lexical forms, which represent grammatical relations, also serve as subcategorization frames; the Completeness and Coherence conditions detect subcategorization violations; relation changing rules can result in a verb having more than one lexical form; and grammatical sentences have a complete and coherent f-structures using one of the verb's forms. Section 1.3 takes a closer look at the rules which create new lexical forms for verbs.

1.3. Relation Changes in LFG

I use the term *relation change* broadly to refer to any change in function-argument association. This includes cases where a given argument ends up with a different function, cases where a given function gets a different non-thematic value, and cases where any change in subcategorization is induced by addition or deletion of an argument from PAS.

Same argument gets a different function. In addition to (1) repeated here as ((13) a), *kick* has a passive lexical form which has different grammatical relations. In contrast to ((13) a), ((13) b) tells us that the patient argument of *kick* is the subject and the agent argument is the OBL_{ag} (oblique agent). This would be appropriate for the sentence *The ball was kicked by someone.*

(13) a.   ($\uparrow$ PRED) = 'kick< agent   patient >'
                                              SUBJ   OBJ

      b.   ($\uparrow$ PRED) = 'kick< agent   patient >'
                                              OBL_{ag} SUBJ

Notice that ((13) b) when used on the sentence *The ball was kicked by someone* will result in *the ball* being interpreted as the patient and *someone* being interpreted as the agent. This is the same as the interpretation achieved by using ((13) a) on the sentence *Someone kicked the ball*. The association of the same phrases with the same thematic roles of the same verb indicates that the two sentences mean roughly the same thing. In this way, LFG captures paraphrase relationships between sentences.

((14) a) and ((14) b) illustrate the effect of another relation changing rule. ((14) a) describes the grammatical relations in *I handed a toy to the baby* where the theme, *a toy*, is the OBJ and the goal, *the baby*, is an OBL_{goal}. ((14) b) represents the grammatical relations in *I handed the baby a toy* where the theme, *a toy* is an OBJ2 while the goal, *the baby*, is the OBJ. Again, both lexical forms result in the same association of phrases to arguments, but those associations are mediated by different grammatical relations.

(14) a.   ($\uparrow$ PRED) = 'hand< agent   theme   goal >'
                                              SUBJ   OBJ OBL_{goal}

      b.   ($\uparrow$ PRED) = 'hand< agent   theme   goal >'
                                              SUBJ   OBJ2   OBJ

Unexpressed Arguments. (15) is yet another lexical form for the verb *kick* which differs from (1), (12), and (13) in that the agent argument is unexpressed. (15) would be appropriate for an agentless passive sentence. Notice that agentless passives have implied or understood agents. *The ball was kicked*, for example, usually means that the ball was kicked by someone.

(15)   ($\uparrow$ PRED) = 'kick< agent   patient >'
                                               Ø   SUBJ

((16) a) and ((16) b) also show an argument alternating between being expressed and being unexpressed. ((16) a) represents the predicate in sentences like *They arrived at the party* while ((16) b) represents the predicate in sentences like *They arrived*. As was the case for the agentless passive, this latter sentence has an understood argument. However, unlike the agentless passive, the understood argument gets a definite interpretation in context like *here* or *there* instead of an indefinite interpretation like *somewhere*.

(16) a. ($\uparrow$ PRED) = 'arrive< theme   goal >'
                          SUBJ   OBL$_{goal}$

　　 b. ($\uparrow$ PRED) = 'arrive< theme   goal >'
                          SUBJ   Ø

Optional Arguments. Some relation changes involve removing an argument from PAS altogether. For example, the sentence *The ship sank* contrasts with *They sank the ship* in that the former has no overtly expressed agent. However, in contrast to an agentless passive like *The ship was sunk*, it has no implied or understood agent either. That is, *The ship sank* does not necessarily mean that there was someone who sank the ship. ((17) a) and ((17) b) are lexical forms for *They sank the ship* and *The ship sank* respectively.

(17) a. ($\uparrow$ PRED) = 'sink< agent   theme >'
                          SUBJ   OBJ

　　 b. ($\uparrow$ PRED) = 'sink< theme >'
                          SUBJ

((18) a) and ((18) b) are also related by the addition/removal of an argument. The sentence *He walked*, which would include ((18) b) as its lexical form, does not necessarily mean that there was somewhere that he walked to. That is, there is not necessarily an implied goal. ((18) a), on the other hand, describes motion toward a goal as in *He walked to school*.

(18) a. ($\uparrow$ PRED) = 'walk< agent   goal >'
                          SUBJ   OBL$_{goal}$

　　 b. ($\uparrow$ PRED) = 'walk< agent >'
                          SUBJ

So far, I have used intuitions about understood arguments to illustrate the difference between optional and unexpressed arguments. In some cases, however, there are more rigorous tests for determining whether an argument is present and unexpressed or not present at all.

For example, an agent argument must be present in order for an instrumental phrase to appear. Therefore, we can use instrumental phrases to detect the presence of implied agent arguments. This test, in fact, confirms our treatment of agentless passives and inchoatives. ((19) a) is ambiguous, it can mean that a torpedo sank along with the ship or it can have an instrumental reading where someone used a torpedo to sink the ship. Since an instrumental phrase occurs in ((19) a), there must be an unexpressed agent. In contrast, ((19) b) is unambiguous. It can only mean that a torpedo sank along with the ship. The absence of an instrumental reading can be attributed to the absence of an agent argument.

(19) a.   The ship was sunk with a torpedo.
    b.   The ship sank with a torpedo.

In Dutch, it is possible to tell whether goal arguments of motion verbs are present and unexpressed or not present at all. Verbs that express motion toward a goal in Dutch take *zijn* (be) as the perfective auxiliary (see section 2.3) while verbs that express motion as a general activity take *hebben* (have). If the presence of a goal argument signifies motion toward a goal, then we can use auxiliary selection to confirm the presence/absence of goal arguments.

The verb *komen* (come) in Dutch always has either an overtly expressed goal or an understood one and always takes *zijn*.

(20) a.   ($\uparrow$ PRED) = 'komen< theme goal >'
                                  SUBJ   OBL$_{goal}$

           Hij is naar school gekomen.
           "He is (i.e. has) come to school."

           *Hij heeft naar school gekomen.
           "He has come to school."

    b.   ($\uparrow$ PRED) = 'komen< theme goal >'
                                  SUBJ   Ø

           Hij is gekomen.
           "He is (i.e. has) come."

           *Hij heeft gekomen.
           "He has come".

Lopen (walk) also takes *zijn* when it has an overtly expressed goal (see ((21) a)). But when there is no overt goal, *lopen* takes either *hebben* or *zijn*. However, *Ik heb gelopen* (I have walked) and *Ik ben gelopen* (I am (i.e. have) walked) mean slightly different things. *Ik heb gelopen* means that I walked around and *Ik ben gelopen* means that I walked to somewhere. The ambiguity of *walk* becomes clear in context: *Ik heb gelopen* could be used in response to the question *What did you do today?* and *Ik ben gelopen* could be used in response to *How did you get here?*

These facts can all be captured with two additional forms for *lopen* — one with an unexpressed goal ((21) b) and one with no goal at all ((21) c). The former expresses directed motion and takes *zijn* as the prefective auxiliary while the latter expresses undirected motion and takes *hebben*.

(21) a.   ($\uparrow$ PRED) = 'lopen$\langle$ agent goal $\rangle$'
                           SUBJ OBL_{goal}

   Hij is naar school gelopen.
   "He is (i.e. has) walked to school."

   *Hij heeft naar school gelopen.
   "He has walked to school."

b.   ($\uparrow$ PRED) = 'lopen$\langle$ agent goal $\rangle$'
                           SUBJ $\emptyset$

   Ik ben gelopen.
   "I am (i.e. have) walked"

c.   ($\uparrow$ PRED) = 'lopen$\langle$ agent $\rangle$'
                           SUBJ

   Ik heb gelopen.
   "I have walked"

Same Function/Different Value. In addition to (2) (repeated here as (23)) which assigns the value ($\uparrow$ XCOMP SUBJ) to the SUBJ function, there is another form of *seem* which assigns a dummy pronoun (*it* in this case) to the SUBJ function by specifying its features — not unexpressed, not locative, and so on. This form represents the grammatical relations in *It seems that people are happy*.

(23)   ($\uparrow$ PRED) = 'seem$\langle$ theme $\rangle$SUBJ'
                               XCOMP

   ($\uparrow$ SUBJ) = ($\uparrow$ XCOMP SUBJ)

(24)   ($\uparrow$ PRED) = 'seem$\langle$ theme $\rangle$SUBJ'
                               COMP

   ($\uparrow$ SUBJ) = $\begin{bmatrix} \text{U} & - \\ \text{LOC} & - \\ \text{NUM sg} \\ \text{PERS 3} \end{bmatrix}$

(24) actually illustrates two relation changes: a change in non-thematic value for the SUBJ function and a change in function (from XCOMP to COMP) for the theme argument.

This section has summarized the different types of relation changing rules. Chapter 2 summarizes some essential properties of relation changing rules and Chapter 3 presents a theory of relation changing rules which accounts for the generalizations presented in Chapters 1 and 2.

Chapter 2
Some Properties of Relation Changing Rules

A theory of relation changing rules, in addition to providing a convenient notation for formulating relation changes, should distinguish possible from impossible relation changes (where possible relation changes are those that are attested in some language) and it should accurately describe different degrees of productivity in relation changing rules. In this chapter, I identify aspects of productivity and possible rules which I will account for in Chapter 3. First, I examine the balance between syntactic productivity and semantic constraints on relation changing rules. Then I turn to a particular class of possible rules which I call the Unaccusative Rules and discuss the insight that these rules provide into the representation of subjects in lexical forms. This leads back to a discussion of the productivity of rules that apply to subjects. This chapter does not constitute a complete inventory of phenomena that a theory of relation changing rules should account for, but it does review many aspects of relation changing rules that have been discussed by Chomsky (1981), Marantz (1984), and Perlmutter (1978).

2.1. Semantic Conditioning of Relation Changing Rules

When talking about relation changing rules, it is useful to distinguish semantically conditioned rules from syntactically productive rules. Syntactically productive rules apply whenever a certain syntactic environment occurs. In LFG, the relevant syntactic environment consists of grammatical functions in lexical forms of verbs. A syntactically productive rule will apply whenever certain functions are present in a lexical form. Semantically conditioned rules, on the other hand, apply to verbs of certain semantic classes or to verbs with certain thematic roles in their PAS.

The distinction between syntactically productive and semantically conditioned processes was pointed out by Wasow (1977, 1980) and Anderson (1977) and has been accepted by many syntacticians. But discussions of relation changing rules rarely acknowledge that an overwhelming majority of relation changing rules are semantically conditioned. (Though this is implicit in work on lexical semantics and case grammar.)

I include here a short list of semantically conditioned relation changes in English. For each rule, I give an example of verbs that undergo the rule, syntactically equivalent verbs which do not undergo the rule, and some idea of what semantic pattern the rule follows.

The Causative/Inchoative Rule relates the (a) and (b) sentences below. Each (a) sentence contains a transitive verb whose subject is an agent and whose object is a theme while each (b) sentence contains an intransitive verb whose subject is a theme.

(25) a.   The movie changed his life.
     b.   His life changed.
(26) a.   The rain filled the pond.
     b.   The pond filled.
(27) a.   The wind turned the windmill.
     b.   The windmill turned.

The Causative/Inchoative Rule cannot be formulated in terms of grammatical functions alone because many verbs which have the same grammatical functions do not undergo the rule. There are many transitive verbs which do not have non-agentive intransitive counterparts and there are many intransitive verbs which cannot become transitive by the addition of an agent (e.g. ((28) a) and ((28) b)).

(28) a.   She talked.
     b.   * They talked her.

The agent-patient verbs ((a) sentences below) are a class of transitive verbs which do not have non-agentive intransitive counterparts. Some agent-patient verbs can be intransitive ((b) sentences) but not as a result of the causative/inchoative rule. When a verb detransitivizes as a result of the causative/inchoative rule, its subject is no longer an agent. Instead, the theme argument, which was the object of the transitive verb, becomes the subject of the intransitive verb. The subjects of intransitive agent-patient verbs, however, are agents. The (c) sentences below are odd because an attempt is made to interpret the subject of an intransitive agent-patient verb as a patient.

(29) a.   Someone kicked the ball.
     b.   The baby kicked.
     c.   * The ball kicked.
         (Cannot mean that someone kicked the ball.)
(30) a.   The hunter shot the bird
     b.   The hunter shot far.
     c.   * The bird shot.
         (Cannot mean that the bird was shot.)
(31) a.   The cook poked the cake.
     b.   * The cook poked.

c.   * The cake poked.
        (Cannot mean that the cake was poked.)

Examples like these show us that it would not be sufficient to describe the causative/inchoative rule in the following way: take a verb which has a SUBJ and OBJ, delete the SUBJ, and change the OBJ to a SUBJ. The problem is that many verbs which have a SUBJ and an OBJ do not undergo the rule (Wasow 1977). Conversely, because of examples like ((28) a) and ((28) b), the rule could not simply take an intransitive verb and make it transtive by adding a subject and making the old subject into a object. The causative/inchoative rule is more naturally described as a rule that applies to a semantic class of verbs rather than to a syntactic class.

The Patient Rule. Hale and Laughren (1983) point out that the patient of an agent-patient verb can appear as an oblique phrase instead of as a direct object ((32) a-(32) c). This is not possible for themes ((33) a-(33) c).

(32) a.   Someone was kicking at the wall.   *agent-patient*
     b.   The hunter shot at the bird.
     c.   Someone was poking at the birthday cake.

(33) a.   * His friends changed at his life.   *agent-theme*
     b.   * The waiter filled at the glasses.
     c.   * The cook turned at the hamburgers.[7]

As was the case with the causative/inchoative rule, the evidence shows that the rule is not syntactically productive. It cannot simply replace OBJ with OBL because there are OBJs which cannot become OBLs.

Theme Expression. Many agent-patient verbs also have the option of expressing the theme (effect) as a direct object while putting the patient in a locative phrase (Hale and Laughren 1983). There is no analogous construction for agent-theme verbs (presumably because a theme cannot be added when there already is one).

(34) a.   I kicked a hole in the wall.   *agent-patient*
     b.   I shot a hole in the wall.
     c.   I poked a hole in the wall.

(35) a.   * I changed a hole in the wall.   *agent-theme*
        (Does not mean that I changed the wall so that it had a hole in it.)
     b.   * The rain filled a flood in the river

---

[7]These are all ungrammatical on the desired readings, though they may have other slightly far-fetched but grammatical readings.

c. * The cook turned a hole in the hamburger.

The Pleonastic *There* Rule. Although it is difficult to precisely characterize the class of intransitive verbs that undergo the pleonastic *there* rule, it is easy to identify semantic classes of verbs which do not undergo the pleonastic *there* rule. For example, verbs that express a change of state do not undergo the rule.

(36) a. A river froze.
     b. * There froze a river.
(37) a. Some butter melted.
     b. * There melted some butter.
(38) a. A sauce thickened.
     b. * There thickened a sauce.

Since it is not true that all intransitive verbs undergo the pleonastic *there* rule, and it is true that the verbs that do not undergo it fall into identifiable semantic classes, it seems that the pleonastic *there* rule is better stated as a semantically conditioned rule than as a syntactically productive one.[8]

Dative Rule. The dative rule is also semantically conditioned. Change of possession verbs which have an OBJ and an OBL_{goal} undergo the rule, but change of location verbs which also have an OBJ and an OBL_{goal} do not undergo the rule.

(39) a. I handed a book to the kids.   *possession*
     b. I handed the kids a book.
(40) a. I sold a book to the kids.   *possession*
     b. I sold the kids a book.
(41) a. I sent a letter to my mother.   *possession*
     b. I sent my mother a letter.
(42) a. I sent a letter to New York.   *location*
     b. * I sent New York a letter.
(43) a. I drove the kids to school.   *location*
     b. * I drove school the kids.   *location*

Passivization. We now begin an extended discussion of a particularly complicated case of semantic conditioning. Each of the six sets of sentences below illustrates a particular pattern. The (b) sentences, which are ungrammatical, are the expected result of passivizing the (a) sentences using an agent phrase. The (c) sentences look like agentless passives of the (a) sentences. And the (d) sentences are alternative sources for the (c) sentences. The question I wish to address is this: are the (c) sentences genuine agentless passives of the (a)

---

[8]Notice that it is not even possible to say that the pleonastic *there* rule is syntactically productive over the class of unaccusative verbs because intransitive change of state verbs appear to be unaccusative in other constructions.

sentences? If they are, then the (a) sentences passivize. But most verbs that have agentless passives also allow their subjects to appear as oblique agents. So the (b) sentences would constitute exceptions of some sort to passivization. I will argue that in fact these are semantic exceptions.

(44) a. The solution involves some changes.
 b. * Some changes are involved by the solution.
 c. Some changes were involved (in the solution).
 d. ? The investigators involved some changes (in the solution).
(45) a. The list includes some interesting items.
 b. * Some interesting items are included by the list.
 c. Some interesting items are included (in the list).
 d. Someone included some interesting items (in the list).
(46) a. The paper requires more work.
 b. * More work is required by the paper.
 c. More work is required (on the paper).
 d. The teacher required more work (on the paper).
(47) a. These languages allow impersonal passives.
 b. * Impersonal passives are allowed by these languages.
 c. Impersonal passivization is allowed (in these languages).
 d. Native speakers allow impersonal passivization (in these languages).
(48) a. This paper calls him a liar.
 b. * He is called a liar by this book.
 c. He is called a liar (in this book).
 d. Someone calls him a liar (in this book).
(49) a. This paper adds something to the paradox.
 b. * Something is added to the paradox by this paper.
 c. Something is added to the paradox.
 d. Someone adds something to the paradox (in this paper).

We must consider three possible analyses of these examples. (1) The (a) sentences passivize but their subjects cannot become OBL_{agent}. (2) The (a) sentences do not passivize at all and the (c) sentences are adjectival passives, not verbal passives of the (a) sentences. (3) The (a) sentences do not passivize and the (c) sentences are passives of the (d) sentences (Granger-Legrand 1983).

It is relatively easy to show that alternative (2) is unsatisfactory. And, although the linguistic evidence makes it difficult to definitively eliminate alternative (3), I will argue that (1) is the hypothesis that best accounts for all these verbs, taken together.

Consider first the possibility that the (c) sentences derive from the (d) sentences. The ungrammaticality of ((44) d) is an obvious problem for this hypothesis and for other examples, there is just a feeling that the active and passive sentences are not related. However, a more rigorous test can be applied to at least one example: the verbs of ((45) a) and ((45) d) can be

2. Syntactic Productivity of Relation Changing Rules

The previous section shows that relation changing rules in general, and Passive in particular, are semantically conditioned. This contrasts sharply with the traditional view of Passive as a paradigmatic syntactic rule. For instance, Wasow (1977,1980) classified the verbal passive as a syntactically productive rule because of the generality with which direct objects can become passive subjects. In applying this criterion of syntactic productivity, Wasow points out that objects with different thematic roles, or with no thematic role at all, can become subjects of passive sentences.

(53) a. A toy was handed to the baby.   *theme*
    b. The baby was handed a toy.   *goal*
    c. The baby was believed to be a good dancer.   *non-thematic*

The purpose of this section is to show that there is a good deal of truth in claims such as this, but that it is subprocesses of Passive that are syntactically productive rather than the rule as a whole. Although Passive is a semantically conditioned rule, it has a syntactically productive component. And, as we will show, the same method of reconciling semantic conditioning with syntactic productivity can be applied to other relation changing rules.

Furthermore, assuming certain general principles, the syntactically productive subrules are predictable from the semantically constrained parts of the rule. For example, suppose that we assume the following principle (Baker 1983).

(54)   **Subject Condition:** Each lexical form must assign a value to the SUBJ function.

Then, once the subject-to-oblique part of Passivization is performed, the object-to-subject part of Passivization must apply. If it did not, and no dummy subject were introduced (section 2.3), the lexical form would not have a subject. (55) shows the passive rule applying in two steps. The intermediate step is unacceptable according to (54).

< agent   theme >   *active*
  SUBJ   OBJ

< agent   theme >   *after SUBJ-to-OBL*
  OBL_{ag} OBJ

< agent   theme >   *after OBJ-to-SUBJ*
  OBL_{ag} SUBJ

(54) also predicts the object-to-subject relation change in other constructions. I will illustrate this using the causative/inchoative rule and the pleonastic *there* rule.

---

shown to belong to different aspectual classes and the aspectual properties of the passive sentence ((45) c) show that it can derive from either active sentence, ((45) a) or ((45) d).

I will now argue that in ((45) a) the verb *include* is a stative verb, while the same verb in ((45) d) is an accomplishment verb (Dowty 1979).

In the morphological simple present tense form, stative verbs are typically used with present tense meaning. They indicate something going on now. Accomplishment verbs, on the other hand, have an unnatural sound in the simple present, and sentences using them in this tense would have to be interpreted as uses of the "historical present."

The list includes an interesting item is stative, and has a straightforward present tense meaning. *She includes an interesting item in the list* is peculiar, and would have to be a case of historical present.

Another test for stativity is the ability to occur in the morphological present progressive. Stative sentences like *The list includes an interesting item* sound odd in the present progressive (e.g., ?*The list is including an interesting item.*) Non-stative sentences like *She includes an interesting item in the list* sound perfectly natural in the present progressive e.g. *She is including an interesting item in the list*.

Notice that in general, aspectual class is not affected by passivization. For instance, stative verbs have stative passives and non-stative verbs have non-stative passives. In order to see this consider the verbs *know* and *kiss*. *Know* is stative: in the simple present, a sentence like *they know the answer* has a real present tense meaning and *they are knowing the answer* sounds odd. *Kiss* is non-stative: in the simple present, *she kisses him* would not be a normal present tense statement; and *she is kissing him* is the natural way to express an event taking place in the present. Like the active verb, the passive of *know* is also stative: *the answer is known* has a present-tense reading and *the answer is being known* sounds odd. The passive of *kiss* is non-stative: *she is kissed* does not have a normal present-tense reading and the real present tense reading is expressed by *she is being kissed*.

Now, stativity can be used to test the source of a sentence like *An interesting item is included (in the list)*. It turns out that this sentence is ambiguous between a stative and a non-stative reading. As it is (in the simple present), it has a real present tense meaning but it can also occur in the present progressive *An interesting item is being included in the list*. One way to account for the ambiguity would be to postulate two corresponding active sentences:

one stative *The list includes an interesting item* and one non-stative *She is including an interesting item in the list*. But before concluding this, we should rule out the possiblity that the stative and non-stative readings of the passive both come from a non-stative active. (Later, I will discuss the possibility that the stative reading is an adjectival passive.)

We can force the passive sentence to be related to the non-stative active sentence *She included an interesting item in the list* by adding the *by*-phrase *by her*. The result is a non-stative sentence *An interesting item is included by her in the list*. This sentence has a historical present reading and the corresponding present progressive sentence has a real present tense reading — *An interesting item is being included by her in the list*. So it seems that only a non-stative passive can come from the non-stative active.

Since, without the *by*-phrase, the sentence *An interesting item is included in the list* has both a stative and a non-stative reading, and since the stative reading cannot come from a non-stative active sentence, the stative reading must come from a stative active sentence like *The list includes an interesting item*.

The stativity test for relatedness cannot be applied to all the examples given here because, for most of the verbs both potential sources of the passive (that is, both the (a) and (d) sentences) are stative.

Now, turning to alternative (2), we consider whether the passives in ((44) c-(49) c) are adjectival or verbal passives. One sufficient test for verb-hood is the ability to take an NP complement (Bresnan 1982a). The passive verb *called* in *I am called a liar in this book* passes this test and, therefore, must be a verb.

I have not conclusively shown that the (c) sentences are related to the (a) sentences by passivization, but I have shown is that some of the passives do not derive from the corresponding (d) sentences and that one of them, at least, is not an adjective. However, even though there is no one verb for which I have shown both things, it is true that the only uniform treatment that would work for all of the verbs above is one which treats the (c) sentences as verbal passives of the (a) sentences.

In theory, the ungrammaticality of the (b) sentences could indicate two things: a general failure of the (a) sentences to passivize or a restriction on the content of OBL_{agent} phrases. But since we claim that the (a) sentences passivize, the ungrammaticality of the (b) sentences can only show that the subjects of the (a) sentences cannot appear in OBL_{agent} phrases.

I claim that the ungrammaticality of the (b) sentences reflects a [...] the $SUBJ$-to-OBL_{agent} relation change which is part of passivization. [...] prepositions as indicators of thematic roles, we would have to conclu[...] the (a) sentences all have the location role: when those arguments app[...] (as they optionally do in the (c) sentences), they are marked by the l[...] and *on*. So, at least for the verbs discussed here, there is a restrict[...] $SUBJ$-to-OBL_{agent} relation change when the SUBJ plays the location ro[...]

A final point about passivization supports the claim that it is [...] apparently transitive sentences do not passivize at all — agent phras[...] These include idiomatic sentences (Bach 1980) and some double obje[...] not have single-object counterparts. In Chapter 4, I will suggest t[...] appear to be transitive fail to passivize for syntactic reasons. Specifica[...] transitive verbs are actually unaccusative. However, I do not believe [...] the examples cited here because of their close relationship to other e[...] verbs which do passivize.

(50) a.   He threw a fit.
     b.   * A fit was thrown by him.
(51) a.   John kicked the bucket.
     b.   * The bucket was kicked by John.
(52) a.   She gave me a headache.
     b.   * She gave a headache to me.
     c.   * I was given a headache by her.

The fact that it has systematic exceptions such as these l[...] thematic rule.

---

[9] I reject the claim (Marantz 1984) that the passive *by*-phrase is a semantic wild-ca[...] role. However, there is clearly more to be said about this issue given that the OBL_{ag} number of different roles.

1. Many diverse points are encompassed by the solution.

2. These things aren't liked by anyone.

3. Nobody was surprised by it.

4. Non-thematic objects can be introduced by syntactic rules.

5. Ten cookies were eaten by the children.

For now, I will suggest that if we had the right definition of agent, it would turn out OBL_{ag} phrases are actually agents.

The causative/inchoative rule, as described above, relates a transitive verb with an agent subject and a theme object to an intransitive verb with a theme subject. This involves two basic relation changes: the agent argument is deleted and the theme argument changes its function from object to subject.

As in passivization, the OBJ-to-SUBJ relation change in the causative/inchoative rule is predictable. If the agent argument is deleted, it can no longer be a SUBJ and the theme argument will have to take on the SUBJ function in order to save the lexical form from violating (54).

(56) < agent theme >   *transitive*
      SUBJ   OBJ

      < theme >   *after removal of agent*
      OBJ

      < theme >   *after OBJ-to-SUBJ*
      SUBJ

Although the causative/inchoative rule was described above as a semantically conditioned rule, we can now see that it consists of two parts: a semantically conditioned part that adds/removes an agent and a syntactically productive part which relates a theme SUBJ to a theme OBJ.[10]

The pleonastic *there* rule is also composed of two relation changes: an argument of the verb alternates between being a SUBJ and being an OBJ while the SUBJ function alternates between being thematic and being non-thematic *there*.

Again, instead of being viewed as a unified semantically constrained rule, the pleonastic *there* rule can be viewed as a composite of a semantically constrained process (introduction of *there* as a dummy subject) and a syntactically productive process (the OBJ-to-SUBJ relation change). Here, the syntactically productive OBJ-to-SUBJ relation change is precictable from the presence or absence of *there*. If the verb does not supply a dummy value for the SUBJ function, some other argument will have to become a SUBJ in order for the lexical form not to violate (54). (57) shows the change in a lexical form from the pleonastic *there* construction to a simple intransitive construction in two steps. The features [U $-$, LOC $+$] in the original lexical form identify pleonastic *there*. Notice that the intermediate stage in the derivation is unacceptable according to (54).

(57)   ⟨ theme ⟩   *with dummy subject*
             OBJ

$$(\uparrow SUBJ) = \begin{bmatrix} U & - \\ LOC & + \end{bmatrix}$$

             ⟨ theme ⟩   *without dummy subject*
             OBJ

             ⟨ theme ⟩   *after OBJ-to-SUBJ*
             SUBJ

The fact that OBJ-to-SUBJ applies as part of both the causative/inchoative rule and the pleonastic *there* rule is further evidence of its syntactic productivity. The pleonastic *there* rule and the causative/inchoative rule apply to some of the same verbs, but there are other verbs

---

[10] Wasow also points out that verbs with non-thematic objects do not undergo the causative/inchoative rule. His explanation for this fact is that the causative/inchoative rule is a lexical rule and lexical rules only apply to arguments with certain thematic roles. In a similar vein, I claim that thematic rules apply to particular semantic classes of verbs and verbs with non-thematic objects are not in the appropriate semantic class to undergo the causative/inchoative rule.

to which one applies and the other does not. For example, change of state verbs undergo the causative/inchoative rule but not the pleonastic *there* rule. The syntactically productive OBJ-to-SUBJ relation change applies to verbs which undergo the pleonastic *there* rule as well as to those that undergo the causative/inchoative rule.

So far, I have shown that relation changing rules can be broken down into basic operations that can be either semantically conditioned or syntactically productive, that some of the operations are predictable from others given certain well-formedness conditions, and that it is the syntactically productive ones that are predictable from the semantically conditioned ones. An additional observation that is incorporated by Chomsky (1981) and Marantz (1984) is that there are very few syntactically productive relation changes.

((58) a) lists what I assume to be the possible syntactically productive operations and ((58) b) lists what I assume to be the allowable semantically conditioned operations. I have given examples where possible. However, I do not know of examples for some of the predicted relation changes.

Notice that ((58) a) is a subset of ((58) b). The double-headed arrows in ((58) a) and ((58) b) indicate that the relation changes are not directional. That is, I do not assume that one grammatical function assignment is more basic than the other. In Chapter 3, I will show how the right and left sides of each relation change below can be derived directly from the predicate argument structure.

(58) a. **Syntactically Productive Operations:**

1. < ... OBJ ... > <---> < ... SUBJ ... >

Example: The OBJ/SUBJ relation change in passivization is syntactically productive.

2. < ... OBJ2 ... > <---> < ... OBJ ... >

Example: Levin (1981), Levin & Simpson (1981) and Zaenen & Maling (1983) show that some Icelandic double object verbs allow both the theme and the goal arguments to become the subject of a passive sentence. They conclude that when the theme passivizes, it is an OBJ and when the goal passivizes, the theme is an OBJ2. This relation change does not occur with all double object verbs and therefore seems at first not to be syntactically productive. However, I will show in Chapter 4 that such a relation change is productive based on argument classification, a notion that I introduce in Chapter 3.

3. < ... OBJ2 ... > <---> < ... SUBJ ... >

Example: Possibly Japanese. In Japanese double object sentences, the theme is marked accusative (o) and the goal is marked dative (ni). When these verbs passivize, the goal becomes the subject and becomes nominative (ga). A possible analysis is that the theme is OBJ and the goal is OBJ2 and it is the OBJ2 which becomes the SUBJ of a passive verb. However, another possible analysis is that the goal is a quirky case marked object as in Icelandic.

4. Assignment of non-thematic values to SUBJ, OBJ, and OBJ2.

Examples: Assignment of an unexpressed dummy subject for Italian passive and unaccusative verbs (Burzio 1981). Also, the Lexical Rule of Functional Control (Section 3.5) productively assigns non-thematic values to SUBJ, OBJ, and OBJ2 based on the subcategorization of the verb.

b. **Semantically Conditioned Operations:**

1. ⟨ ... OBJ ... ⟩ ⟨---⟩ ⟨ ... SUBJ ... ⟩

   Example: Certain idiosyncratic alternations: *This benefits/profits me.~I benefit/profit from this.*[11]

2. ⟨ ... OBJ2 ... ⟩ ⟨---⟩ ⟨ ... OBJ ... ⟩

3. ⟨ ... OBJ2 ... ⟩ ⟨---⟩ ⟨ ... SUBJ ... ⟩

4. Assigment of non-thematic values to SUBJ, OBJ, and OBJ2.

   Example: The pleonastic *there* rule in English is semantically conditioned.

5. Addition/deletion of arguments.

   Example: The causative/inchoative rule.

6. ⟨ ... OBL ... ⟩ ⟨---⟩ ⟨ ... SUBJ ... ⟩

   Example: I claim that the SUBJ/OBL relation change in passivization is semantically conditioned. Also, there are various idiosyncratic SUBJ/OBL relation changes: *This benefits me/I benefit from this, The landlord rented the apartment to the tennant/The tennant rented the apartment from the landlord.*

7. ⟨ ... OBL ... ⟩ ⟨---⟩ ⟨ ... OBJ ... ⟩

   Example: The dative rule and the patient rule.

8. ⟨ ... OBL ... ⟩ ⟨---⟩ ⟨ ... OBJ2 ... ⟩

9. ⟨ ... ∅ ... ⟩ ⟨---⟩ ⟨ ... SUBJ ... ⟩

10. ⟨ ... ∅ ... ⟩ ⟨---⟩ ⟨ ... OBJ ... ⟩

    Example: Unspecified object deletion: *The children ate dinner/The children ate.*

11. ⟨ ... ∅ ... ⟩ ⟨---⟩ ⟨ ... OBJ2 ... ⟩

((58) a) and ((58) b) show an inventory of possible syntactically productive and semantically conditioned relation changes. But it may be the case that not all languages have

---

[11] It may seem that *me* is not really an OBJ in the first of these sentences because the sentence does not passivize. However, in Chapter 4, I will show that there are circumstances under which transitive verbs do not passivize, namely, when they have two general unrestricted arguments (see Chapter 4).

all of these operations. For example, there is no evidence that American English has the OBJ-to-OBJ2 relation change.

The division between syntactically productive and semantically conditioned rules depends on the division between semantically unrestricted functions (SUBJ, OBJ, and OBJ2) and semantically restricted functions (the oblique functions). Syntactically productive processes can only replace one unrestricted function with another or assign non-thematic values to unrestricted functions. This is discussed further in Chapter 3.

Notice that some operations are on both lists. This indicates that a given operation can be syntactically productive in one language and semantically conditioned in another. Assignments of non-thematic dummy values to the SUBJ function are like this: *there*-insertion is semantically constrained in English but selection of dummy subjects in Italian seems to apply productively over the syntactic class of unaccusative verbs (Burzio 1981, Rosen 1981).

2.3. Unaccusative Rules

Unaccusative Rules (URs) are rules which refer to two types of subjects. The set of *canonical subjects* includes subjects of transitive verbs while the set of *non-canonical subjects* includes subjects of passive verbs. Subjects of intransitive verbs are split between the two types: some of them act like subjects of transitive verbs with respect to URs and others act like subjects of passive verbs. In addition, some URs treat raising-to-subject verbs, reflexive verbs, and verbs with dummy subjects as if they had non-canonical subjects and some URs treat objects of transitive verbs like non-canonical subjects.

Notice that URs support Perlmutter's (1978) Unaccusative Hypthesis by identifying the need for two types of intransitive verb. Following Perlmutter, I use the term *unaccusative verb* for intransitive verbs with non-canonical subjects and the term *unergative verb* for intransitive verbs with canonical subjects.

(59) summarizes the distinctions made by URs. I will illustrate these distinctions with examples from English and Dutch.

(59) CANONICAL SUBJECTS:

subjects of transitive verbs

subjects of some intransitive verbs (unergative verbs)

NON-CANONICAL SUBJECTS:

subjects of passive verbs

subjects of other intransitive verbs (unaccusative verbs)

sometimes, subjects of raising-to-subject verbs

sometimes, subjects of reflexive verbs

sometimes, dummy subjects

(Note: Some URs group objects of transitive verbs with the non-canonical subjects.)

2.3.1. Resultative Secondary Predication.

The examples in (60) illustrate Resultative Secondary Predication (RSP).[12] Each sentence contains a secondary predicate (italicized) which is predicated of another element in the sentence (underlined). For example, *flat* in (60) a is predicated of *nail*. Furthermore, the secondary predicate expresses a state that results from the event described by the verb. In (60) a, *flat* is the state of the nail which results from hammering.

(60) a. He hammered the nail *flat*.
 b. He tore it *to pieces*.
 c. He wiped it *clean*.

Resultative Secondary predicates differ from secondary state predicates which describe a state that is simultaneous with the event described by the verb. *Unopened*, for example, in *The package arrived unopened* is a secondary state predicate. It describes the state of the package *when* it arrived rather than describing a state of the package that *resulted from* arriving. Secondary state predication seems to be a different process from resultative secondary predictation and will not be discussed here. (See Simpson (1983b), Halliday (1967), and Rothstein (1983) for discussion of secondary state predication.)

Simpson (1983a) points out that resultative secondary predicates (henceforth

---

[12] See Simpson (1983a), Halliday (1967), Dowty (1979), and Randall (1983) for discussion of this construction.

resultatives) can be predicated of objects of transitive verbs (examples above), subjects of passive verbs ((61) a-(61) c), and subjects of some intransitive verbs ((62) a-(62) c). Notice that none of these things are canonical subjects according to (59).

(61) a.   The nail was hammered *flat*.
     b.   It had been torn *to pieces*.
     c.   It was wiped *clean*.
(62) a.   The vase broke *to pieces*.
     b.   The lake froze *solid*.
     c.   The cookies burned *to a crisp*.

Simpson also points out that resultatives are never predicated of subjects of transitive verbs. So, ((63) a) cannot mean that I become exhausted as a result of hammering. Furthermore, some intransitive verbs do not allow resultatives to be predicated of their subjects ((64) a-(64) c). The subjects which cannot control resultatives are canonical subjects.

(63) a.   * I hammered the nail *exhausted*.
     b.   * I broke it *to tears*.
     c.   * The oven burnt the cookies *dirty*.
(64) a.   * The baby cried *to sleep*.
     b.   * They ate *sick*.
     c.   * The speaker talked *hoarse*.

Sentences such as ((64) a-(64) c) can be saved by inserting a *fake reflexive* object to control the resultative predicate but syntactically, these sentences are syntactically equivalent to ((60) a-(60) c) where an OBJ controls the predicate.

(65) a.   The baby cried himself *to sleep*.
     b.   They ate themselves *sick*.
     c.   The speaker talked himself *hoarse*.

Notice that Resultative Secondary Predication illustrates the pattern in (59) in that it distinguishes subjects of transitive verbs (which cannot control resultatives) from subjects of passives (which can control resultatives). It also splits intransitive verbs into two classes: those whose subjects can control resultatives (like passive verbs) and those whose subjects cannot control resultatives (like transitive verbs).

The pattern in (59) is significant for the theory of grammatical relations. We cannot simply say that resultatives are predicated of subjects and objects because not all subjects can control resultatives. In order to formulate resultative secondary predication (and other URs) we must establish a representation of grammatical relations which includes two types of subjects.[13] However, at the same time, we need to maintain the ability to formulate rules which *do* apply uniformly to all subjects.

2.3.2. The Pleonastic *there* Construction

The pleonastic *there* construction in English is also the result of a UR. This rule applies to some intransitive verbs ((66) a-(66) b) but it does not apply to other intransitive verbs ((67) a-(67) b) or to active transitive verbs ((68) a-(68) c).

(66) a.   A discussion followed.
     b.   There followed a discussion.
(67) a.   A child cried.
     b.   * There cried a child.
(68) a.   A discussion followed the movie.
     b.   * There followed the movie a discussion.
     c.   * There followed a discussion the movie.

Futhermore, the pleonastic *there* rule does seem to apply to passive verbs. Consider ((69) a) and ((69) b). I claim that there are two possible analyses of ((69) b): (1) that it is related to ((69) a) by a stylistic (non-relation changing) rule and (2) that its grammatical relations are different from those in ((69) a). Assuming that direct objects in English immediately follow the verb and that the postposed NP in a pleonastic *there* sentence is an OBJ, I claim that ((69) a) is the result of applying the pleonastic *there* rule to the lexical form of *be*. In this case, *a battle* is the OBJ of a special form of *be*. ((69) b) could be the result of applying heavy NP shift to ((69) a) or it could be the result of applying the pleonastic *there* rule to the lexical form of the passive verb *enacted*. *A battle* in this case is the OBJ of *enacted*.

(69) a.   There *was a battle* about to be enacted between two leaders.
     b.   There was about to be *enacted a battle between two leaders*.
(70) a.   On the board, there *was a message* written announcing the time and date of the exam.
     b.   On the board, there was *written a message* announcing the time and date of the exam.[14]

---

[13] Perlmutter would take URs as evidence for a more general phenomenon: the need for multiple levels of representation and the need for several types of subject. See Perlmutter (1982).

[14] Some sentences with this word order sound very awkward for reasons that I don't understand. The lack of robustness could indicate that the process in question is, in fact, a stylistic rule. But it could also indicate that it is a delicate semantically conditioned relation change.

2.3.3. Passivization in Dutch

Passivization in Dutch is a UR. It applies to transitive verbs ((71) a) and to some intransitive verbs. But, as noted in Perlmutter (1978), it does not apply to all intransitive verbs.

(71) a. Hij wast het raam.
"He washes the window."
b. Het raam *wordt* door hem gewassen.
"The window is washed by him."

(72) a. De jongelui dansen hier vaak.
"The young people dance here often."
b. Er wordt hier door de jongelui vaak gedanst.
"It is danced here often by the young people"

(73) a. Men slaapt vaak in deze kamer.
"People sleep often in this room."
b. Er wordt in deze kamer vaak geslapen. (P 35)
"It is often slept in this room"

(74) a. Men spreekt/praat/denkt vaak over dit probleem.
"People speak/talk/think often about this problem."
b. Over dit probleem wordt vaak gesproken/gepraat/gedacht.
"About this problem it is often spoken/talked/thought."

(75) a. Men niest/hoest.
"People sneeze/cough."
b. Er wordt geniesd/gehoest/gehikt. (P 42)
"It is (being) sneezed/coughed/hiccoughed."

(76) a. De lijken rotten weg.
"The corpses rotted away."
b. * Door de lijken werd al gerot. (P 51a)
"By the corpses it was already rotted."

(77) a. De kinderen verdwijnen uit dit weeshuis.
"The children disappear from this orphanage."
b. * Uit dit weeshuis wordt (er) door vele kinderen verdwenen. (P 61a)
"From this orphanage it is disappeared by many children"

(78) a. Zulke dingen gebeurden hier nooit.
"Such things never happened here."
b. * Hier werd er door zulke dingen nooit gebeurd. (P 65b)
"Here it was never happened by such things"

Passivization, of course, does not appy to already passive verbs. If it did, it would have the same effect that it has on other intransitive verbs; the subject of the active sentence would optionally appear in a *door*-phrase and the dummy subject *er* would be inserted. (79) is an attempt to passivize ((71) b). Notice that (79) does not double the auxiliary of the morphology in ((71) b). This is because the auxiliary and the morphology that accompany the passive are not part of the passive rule in LFG. So, applying the passive rule twice would not result in a doubling of these things.

(79)   * Er wordt gewassen door het raam.
         "It is washed by the window."
         Cannot mean that the window is getting washed.

Perlmutter and Postal (1984) used the unpassivizability of certain verbs to support their 1-Advancement Exclusiveness Law. I take these examples simply to show that we need a representation of grammatical relations which clearly separates verbs with canonical subjects from verbs with non-canonical subjects. Passivization must be formulated so that it applies to the former and not to the latter.

2.3.4. Experiencer Inversion

There is a set of Dutch verbs which allow two basic word orders for their arguments. In each (a) sentence below, a nominative NP precedes the tensed verb and a non-nominative NP (henceforth the *experiencer*) follows it. (This construction has also been discussed by den Besten (1982), Safir (1982), and Hoekstra (1984).) I will refer to the (a) sentences as *uninverted* and to the (b) sentences as *inverted*. In both the (a) and the (b) sentences, the verb agrees with the nominative NP.

(80) a. Deze boeken$_{nom.\ pl.}$ bevallen$_{pl.}$ hem$_{dat.\ sg.}$.
         these books   please   him
         "These books please him./He enjoys these books."
   b.   Hem$_{dat.\ sg.}$ bevallen$_{pl.}$ deze boeken.
         him   please   these books
         "These books please him./He enjoys these books."

(81) a. Dit overkomt hem.
         this happens him
         "This happens to him."
   b.   Hem overkomt dit.
         him happens this
         "This happens to him."

(82) a. De jurk past mij.
         "The dress fits me."
   b.   Mij past de jurk.
         me fits the dress
         "The dress fits me."

The word order in inverted sentences is exactly what one would expect from topicalizing the (a) sentences. Since the tensed verb in main clauses must stay in second position and the topicalized element must be initial, the subject of a topicalized sentence must appear after the tensed verb. Of course, the verb still agrees with the subject which now follows it.

(83) a. Hij zal de appels wel opeten. *untopicalized*
   He will the apples surely eat.
   "He will eat the apples."
 b. De appels zal hij wel opeten. *topicalized*
   The apples will he surely eat.
   "The apples, he'll eat"

Although it looks on the surface like inverted sentences could be topicalizations of the uninverted ones, this possibility must be rejected because inverted sentences differ distributionally in two ways from topicalized sentences. First, topicalized clauses cannot be embedded while inverted clauses can be embedded.

(84) a. Ik denk dat hij de appels wel zal opeten. *untopicalized*
   I think that he the apples surely will eat.
   "I think that he will eat the apples."
 b. * Ik denk dat de appels hij zal opeten. *topicalization*
   I think that the apples he will eat.
   "I think that, the apples, he'll eat."
(85) a. Ik denk dat dat me is overkomen. *uninverted*
   I think that that me happened is
   "I think that that has happened to me."
 b. Ik denk dat me dat is overkomen. *inverted*
   I think that me that is happened
   "I think that that has happened to me."

Second, in yes-no questions, the tensed verb inverts with the first NP. This is possible when the first NP is a fronted experiencer but not when the first NP is a topic.

(86) a. Zal hij de appels wel opeten? *untopicalized*
   "Will he eat the apples?"
 b. * Zal de appels hij wel opeten? *topicalization*
   "Will he eat the apples?"
(87) a. Zullen deze boeken u bevallen? *uninverted*
   "Will these books please you?"
 b. Zullen u deze boeken bevallen? *inverted*
   "Will these books please you?"

Having shown that experiencer inversion is not topicalization, I will now show that experiencer inversion is a relation changing rule which applies to verbs with non-canonical subjects. In order to do this, I will show that any active verb which passivizes cannot undergo experiencer inversion, that experiencer inversion verbs do not passivize, and that there are passive verbs which undergo experiencer inversion.

In the last subsection I showed that passivization applies to verbs with canonical subjects. If experiencer inversion applies to verbs with non-canonical subjects, then there should not be any verbs which passivize and undergo experiencer inversion. The next set of examples supports this prediction. *Haten* (hate) and *bewonderen* (admire) passivize and do not undergo experiencer inversion (that is, the experiencer must be nominative and initial in the clause) while *bevallen* (please/enjoy) and *overkomen* (happen) undergo experiencer inversion (examples above) and do not passivize. ((90) a-(91) b) are attempts to passivize inversion verbs. ((90) a) and ((91) a) are attempts to passivize inverted sentences while ((90) b), ((90) c) and ((91) b) are attempts to passivize uninverted sentences. Notice that ((91) b) may be grammatical but only with a shift in the meaning of *overkomen* from *happen* to *overcome*.

(88) a. Ik haat het.
"I hate it."
 b. Het haat mij. *no inversion*
"It hates me."
Only ok if *het* is animate. Cannot mean that *I hate it*.
 c. Huiswerk wordt gehaat door iedereen. *passive*
"Homework is hated by eveyone."
(89) a. Ik bewonder het.
"I admire it."
 b. Het bewondert mij. *no inversion*
"It admires me."
Only ok if *het* is animate. Cannot mean that *I admire it*.
 c. Het wordt door mij bewonderd. *passive*
"It is admired by me."
(90) a. * Het wordt bevallen.
it was enjoyed/pleased
 b. * Mij wordt bevallen.
me was pleased
 c. * Ik wordt bevallen.
I was pleased
(91) a. * Het wordt overkomen.
it was happened
 b. Ik ben overkomen door angst.
"I am overcome by angst."
Note that this is not a passive of the inversion sense of the verb.

Furthermore, if experiencer inversion were a UR, we might expect to find passive verbs which undergo the rule. This too turns out to be true (den Besten 1982). In each set of sentences below, the (a) sentence is a passive with an initial nominative NP bearing the theme role and the (b) sentence is also a passive of the same verb with an initial non-nominative NP bearing the goal role. The (c) through (f) sentences show that the (a) and (b) sentences are not instances of topicalization by showing that they can occur in embedded clauses and that the initial NP can invert with the tensed verb in yes-no questions. The analysis of experiencer inversion in Chapter 5 handles the alternation between the (a) and (b) sentences below as well as the alternation between inverted and uninverted active sentences.[15]

(92) a. De urn is mijn oom geschonken.
the urn is my uncle given
"The urn was given to my uncle."
b. Mijn oom is de urn geschonken.
my uncle is the urn given
"My uncle was given the urn."
c. Is de urn mijn oom geschonken?
is the urn my uncle given
"Was the urn given to my uncle?"
d. Is mijn oom de urn geschonken?
is my uncle the urn given
"Was my uncle given the urn?"
e. Ik denk dat de urn mijn oom geschonken is.
I think that the urn my uncle given is
"I think that the urn was given to my uncle."
f. Ik denk dat mijn oom de urn geschonken is.
I think that my uncle the urn given is
"I think that my uncle was given the urn."

(93) a. De urn is mijn oom overhandigd.
the urn is my uncle given
"The urn was given to my uncle."
b. Mijn oom is de urn overhandigd.
my uncle is the urn given
"My uncle was given the urn."
c. Is de urn mijn oom overhandigd?
is the urn my uncle given
"Was the urn given to my uncle?"
d. Is mijn oom de urn overhandigd?.
is my uncle the urn given
"Was my uncle given the urn?"
e. Ik denk dat de urn mijn oom overhandigd is.
I think that the urn my uncle given is
"I think that the urn was given to my uncle."
f. Ik denk dat mijn oom de urn overhandigd is.
I think that my uncle the urn given is
"I think that my uncle was given the urn."

---

[15]Notice that it is not clear where the subjects of experiencer inversion verbs fit into the definition of canonical subject. The problem is that in their non-inverted form, experiencer inversion verbs look like transitive verbs but according to the chart in (59) transitive verbs have canonical subjects. So, either experiencer inversion verbs are not really transitive or they are an exceptional type of transitive verb with non-canonical subjects. I return to this issue in Chapters 4 and 5 where I suggest that the latter is true.

2.3.5. Auxiliary Selection

Many languages have a past tense construction consisting of a past participle and an auxiliary verb corresponding to English *have*.

(94) a. I have telephoned John. — English
b. J'ai telephone a Jean. — French
    I have telephoned to Jean.
c. Giovanni ha telefonato. — Italian
    Giovanni has telephoned.
d. Hun hefur kysst Olaf. — Icelandic
    She has kissed Olaf.
e. Hij heeft geslapen. — Dutch
    He has slept.
f. Nik liburua ekarri dut. — Basque
    I book bring 3sgOBJ-UKAN(have)-1sgSUBJ.
    I have brought the book.

This construction differs in interpretation from language to language, but whatever it means, it is common in languages which exhibit this construction to find a class of intransitive verbs which use the copula, corresponding to English *be*, in place of *have*.

(95) a. Il est arrive. — French
    He is arrived.
b. Giovanni e arrivato. — Italian
    Giovanni is arrived.
c. Hann er kominn. — Icelandic
    He is arrived.
d. Hij is ingeslapen. — Dutch
    He is fallen asleep.
e. Ni etorri naiz. — Basque
    I come 1sgSUBJ-IZAN(be)
    I am come

In Dutch, the two aspectual auxiliaries are *hebben* (have) and *zijn* (be). I will use the term *hebben*-verbs for verbs that take *hebben* and *zijn*-verbs for verbs that take *zijn*.

Studies of auxiliary selection in Italian (Burzio 1981, Rosen 1981) and Basque (B. Levin 1983) have shown that it is an unaccusative rule in those languages: transitive verbs and unergative verbs take *have* while unaccusative and passive verbs (among other things) take *be*. However, the situation is less clear in Dutch because although auxiliary selection seems to exemplify the distinction between canonical and non-canonical subjects with non-canonical subjects triggering the presence of *zijn*, the *zijn*-verbs do not have the usual semantic characteristics of unaccusative verbs. Furthermore, many *zijn* verbs passivize as if they were unergative and many verbs which act unaccusative in that they do not passivize do not take *zijn*. In other words, passivization and auxiliary selection do not agee on which verbs are unaccusative.

While this type of discrepancy would be problematic for many theories, I take it to be *typical* of URs. In Chapter 5, I suggest that many apparent URs are actually defined partly or totally in terms of semantic classes and thematic roles instead of being defined in terms of the syntactic classes of unaccusative and unergative verbs. Such rules appear to be URs because the semantic distinctions that they are sensitive to are very close to the semantic distinctions that separate the syntactic classes of unaccusative and unergative verbs. In Chapter 5, I show that we can resolve the discrepancy between auxiliary selection and passivization by formulating auxiliary selection partly in terms of semantic classes and partly in terms of the syntactic distinction between unaccusative and unergative verbs. Here, I will simply present the evidence that Dutch auxiliary selection fits the pattern in (59) and therefore deserves to be called a UR.

In order to show that Dutch auxiliary selection is a UR, I will show that intransitive verbs are split between taking *hebben* and taking *zijn*, that some experiencer inversion verbs are *zijn*-verbs, that all other transitive verbs are *hebben*-verbs, and that passive verbs are *zijn*-verbs. People who are familiar with Dutch will find only the first two of these points to be obviously true. The other points will require some discussion.

Intransitive *hebben* and *zijn*-verbs. Auxiliary selection clearly splits the intransitive verbs into two classes. One class can occur with *hebben* and not *zijn* while the other class can occur with *zijn* and not *hebben*.

(96) a. De kinderen zijn in Amsterdam gebleven. *zijn*
the children are in Amsterdam remained
"The children have remained in Amsterdam."
b. * De kinderen hebben in Amsterdam gebleven. *hebben*
the children have in Amsterdam remained
"The children have remained in Amsterdam."
(97) a. * Hij is gewerkd.
he is worked
"He has worked." *zijn*
b. Hij heeft gewerkd.
he has worked
"He has worked." *hebben*

Some verbs appear to take either auxiliary, but it turns out that the circumstances under which they take *hebben* are quite different from the circumstances under which they take *zijn*. For example, in Chapter 1, I showed that certain motion verbs have to take *zijn* when they have an overt directional complement or an unexpressed directional complement, but they have to take *hebben* when they have a non-directional reading.

(98) a. Ik ben naar school gelopen. *zijn*
I am to school walked
"I have walked to school."
b. * Ik heb naar school gelopen. *hebben*
I have to school walked
"I have walked to school."
c. Ik heb gelopen. *hebben*
"I have walked."
d. Ik ben gelopen. *zijn*
I am walked
"I have walked (to some place)."

Furthermore, I showed in Chapter 1 that the directed readings of these motion verbs reflect the presence of an optional goal argument. Each of these verbs, therefore has two different predicate argument structures: one with a goal argument and one without.

(99) a. < agent goal > *directed motion*
b. < agent > *non-directed motion*

Although motion verbs themselves take either auxiliary, each of their predicate argument structures takes only one auxiliary. The PAS which contains a goal takes only *zijn* and the PAS which does not contain a goal takes only *hebben*. I am assuming that each different lexical form constitutes a separate lexical entry. Therefore, if we take *verb* to mean *lexical entry*, then it is true that auxiliary selection assigns a unique auxiliary to each intransitive verb. Thus, auxiliary selection, like other unaccusative rules, identifies two distinct classes of intransitive verbs.

Experiencer Inversion Verbs. Experiencer inversion verbs, like intransitive verbs, fall into two classes: those that take *zijn* ((100) a-(100) b) and those that take *hebben* ((101) a-(101) c). This may seem surprising in light of the claim that all experiencer inversion verbs have non-canonical subjects. However, there is a simple account of these facts: those that take *zijn* support the claim that *zijn*-verbs have non-canonical subjects and those that take *hebben* simply show that while having a non-canonical subject is a necessary condition for selection of *zijn*, it is not sufficient.

(100)a. Het is mij bevallen.
It have pleased me."
b. Het is hem overkomen.
"It has happened to him."

(101)a. Het heeft u berouwd.
"You have regretted it."
b. Het heeft ons vreemd aangedaan.
"It has struck us as odd."
c. Het heeft een boel gekost.
"It cost a lot."

Transitive verbs. Although it is generally true that transitive verbs do not take *zijn*, there are some apparent exceptions which must be dealt with before we can solidly assert this. The list below is taken from Donaldson (1981).

(102)a. Hij is een zaak in de stad begonnen.
He is a business in the town begun.
"He has begun a business in the town."
b. Ik ben mijn gedicht vergeten.
I am my poem forgotten.
"I have forgotten my poem."
c. De buurman is hem gevolgd.
the neighbor is him followed.
"The neighbor has followed him."
d. Ik ben het Frans geheel verleerd.
I am French totally forgotten.
"I have totally forgotten French."
e. Ik ben hem op straat tegengekomen.
I am him on the street bumped-into.
"I have bumped into him on the street."
f. Juliana is haar moeder in 1948 opgevolgd.
Juliana is her mother in 1948 followed.
"Juliana (has) succeeded her mother in 1948."

Although judgements vary from informant to informant and from day to day, it appears that some of the verbs in ((102) a-(102) f) do not passivize. I will take this as an indication that, like the experiencer inversion verbs, they do not have canonical subjects. (In Chapter 4, I will present an analysis of transitive verbs with non-canonical subjects.) The verbs that do not passivize are *tegenkomen* (bump into) and *vergeten* (forget (a fact, a poem)). (*Vergeten* has another meaning, forget about something/leave something behind, in which it takes *hebben* and passivizes.)

The remaining verbs in ((102) a-(102) f) do, in fact, passivize and therefore seem like they might be counterexamples to the claim that only verbs with non-canonical subjects take *zijn*. However, in contrast to most verbs which take one auxiliary or the other, those verbs all alternate between taking *hebben* and taking *zijn* as the aspectual auxiliary. This could indicate that the verbs are syntactically ambiguous between having a canonical subject and having a non-canonical subject. When they have a non-canonical subject, they take *zijn* and when they have a canonical subject, they take *hebben* and passivize.

I conclude that there are no convincing counterexamples to the claim that verbs with canonical subjects do not take *zijn*.

Passive Verbs. At first it seems that passive verbs and past participles of unaccusative verbs do not select the same auxiliary in Dutch. *Zijn* is the auxiliary that occurs with *zijn*-verbs to express perfective aspect but *worden* is the basic auxiliary of the passive construction in the simple present and past tense.

(103) a.   De kinderen *zijn* naar huis gelopen.   *perfective unaccusative*
           "The children have walked home."
    b.   Het raam *wordt* door hem gewassen.   *passive*
           "The window is washed by him."

However, a puzzling fact about Dutch passives is that there are two ways of expressing perfective aspect. The most obvious is to embed *worden*, which is a *zijn*-verb, under *zijn*, the perfective auxiliary of *zijn*-verbs. The result is shown in ((104) a) but people rarely say this (Donaldson 1981, p. 162). Instead, they say ((104) b) where *worden* has been "dropped".

(104) a.   Het raam is door hem gewassen geworden.
           the window is by him washed been.
           "The window has been washed."
    b.   Het raam is door hem gewassen.
           "The window is by him washed."

A simple account of ((104) a) and ((104) b) arises from the analysis of passivization and AUX-selection proposed here. Passive participles, which are created in the lexicon, enter into various periphrastic constructions in c-structure and f-structure. The construction *worden* + passive participle is interpreted as a simple present/past tense construction, ((103) b). Furthermore, since *worden* is a *zijn*-verb, the way to perfectivize it is to embed it under *zijn*, ((104) a).

((104) b) results from the fact that *worden* is not an inherent part of the passive construction. In LFG (and Relational Grammar) passivization is seen as an operation on the grammatical relations of a verb (Bresnan 1982a). The fact that passive verbs appear in construction with an auxiliary verb is not part of the passive rule, but a consequence the distribution of tensed, infinitival, and participial forms of verbs. For example, main clauses do not allow participial main verbs, and hence the passive participal must appear embedded under tensed verb. Similarly, the verb *stop* in English requires present participles as complements, and hence passive verbs must appear embedded under *being* in complements of *stop* (*They stopped being robbed/*They stopped robbed*). Evidence that the copula construction is not part of the passive rule comes from the fact that passive verb phrases often appear as adjuncts without the copula (*Cars owned by rich people are often quite elaborate*, *Admired by her friends, Jane had no reason to worry*). Separating the passive rule from the syntactic construction with the copula allows for the general distribution of passive verbs in various syntactic contexts.

Worden is not an inherent part of the passive construction. Its function is simply to carry tense (or other morphological/syntactic properties) in main clauses (or other syntactic contexts). Passive verbs might just as well be embedded under *zijn* which could also serve this function. Hence the existence of ((104) b).

An alternative account of ((104) a) and ((104) b) could be based on the assumption that *worden* is absent phonologically, but is present functionally in ((104) b). That is, although c-structure, the input to phonological interpretation and production, does not contain *worden*, *worden* could be built into f-structure, which is input to semantic interpretation, via functional equations associated with *zijn*. This would account for the truth-conditional equivalence of ((104) b) and ((104) a), but would be unnecessarily complicated.

Donaldson (p. 162) points out that the truth-conditional equivalence of ((104) a) and ((104) b) follows from a simple implicature: if the window has been washed then it is washed. This makes it possible to maintain the simple generalization that passive verbs can be embedded directly under *zijn* without resorting to an "invisible *worden*" solution.

Before concluding that *zijn* is the aspectual auxiliary of passive verbs, one additional consideration must be dealt with. As in English, passive participles in Dutch can serve as adjectives. If *gewassen* in ((104) b) were an adjective and not a passive verb, it would seem that passive verbs do not take *zijn* and we would have a much weaker case for claiming that auxiliary selection is a UR.

Two pieces of evidence show that *gewassen* in ((104) b) is a verb and not an adjective. First, it appears with an agent phrase *door hem* (by him). Second, adjectives, in general, refer to states rather than to events that take place at particular times. As a result, they cannot be modified by phrases like *vier keer* (four times). Although the participle *gewassen* can be an adjective with a stative reading, it can also have a non-stative reading which can be accompanied by modifiers like *vier keer*.

(105)   Het raam is vier keer gewassen.
         "The window has been washed four times."

In short, I have shown that Dutch auxiliary selection illustrates the distinction between canonical and non-canonical subjects: transitive verbs do not take *zijn*, passive verbs do take *zijn*, experiencer inversion verbs take *zijn* and intransitive verbs split into two classes, those that take *zijn* an those that take *hebben*.

2.4. SUBJs and OBJs

So far, I have discussed three properties of relation changing rules: semantic conditioning, syntactic productivity, and sensitivity to two types of subject. A fourth phenomenon for a theory of relation changing rules to account for is an imbalance in the distribution of SUBJs and OBJs. Almost all arguments which are objects in some sentence are subjects in a related sentence, but the reverse is not true. There are many arguments which are subjects in some sentence and are not objects in any related sentence.

To see this, consider the following examples where the (a) and (b) sentences are related by relation changing rules. The argument which is an OBJ in each (a) sentence is a SUBJ in the corresponding (b) sentence.

(106)a.   Someone kicked the ball.
    b.   The ball was kicked.
(107)a.   They sank the ship.
    b.   The ship sank.
(108)a.   There followed a discussion.
    b.   A discussion followed.
(109)a.   Hem bevallen deze boeken.
             him please these books
             "He enjoys these books./ These books please him."
    b.   Deze boeken bevallen hem.
             these books please him
             "He enjoys these books./ These books please him."

In contrast, there are many arguments which are subjects in some sentence but are not ever assigned to the OBJ function by any relation changing rule. For example, there are no relation changing rules which assign the OBJ function to the arguments which are subjects in ((110) a) and ((110) b).

(110)a.   Someone threw/took/caught/kicked the ball.
    b.   Someone talked/worked/cried/played.

Notice that it is the canonical subjects (subjects of transitive and unergative verbs) which never show up as objects. The arguments which are subjects of passive verbs, unaccusative verbs, and experiencer inversion verbs, on the other hand, can be objects.

An obvious way to account for the imbalance between subjects and objects is to have relation changes be directional and to say that OBJs can become subjects but subjects cannot become objects. However, if relation changes are not directional there must be some other way of allowing some subjects to be objects while preventing other subjects from doing so. In Chapter 3, I show how to account for the imbalance in a non-directional theory of relation changing rules.

Chapter 3
A Theory of Relation Changing Rules

In Chapter 2, I discussed four properties of relation changing rules: semantic conditioning, syntactic productivity, sensitivity to two types of subject, and apparent directionality of the OBJ/SUBJ relation change. In this chapter, I present a theory of relation changing rules which models these properties.

The theory is based on an enriched representation of grammatical relations in which thematic arguments are grouped into classes before grammatical functions are assigned. Relation changes result either from *reclassifying* arguments or from assigning a different function to a classified argument.

LFG with Argument Classification (AC) captures the four properties of relation changing rules which I discussed in the last chapter: most semantically conditioned relation changes result from alternate class assignments to the same argument; syntactically productive relation changes result from alternate grammatical function assignments to the same classified argument and since principles of the theory tightly constrain the possibilities for assigning functions to classified arguments, there are few allowable syntactically productive operations and they are, for the most part, predictable from the argument classifications; the theory provides for two types of subject required by unaccusative rules because the SUBJ function can be assigned to arguments of two different classes and unaccusative rules are sensitive to argument classifications instead of or in addition to grammatical functions; and finally, the directionality of the OBJ/SUBJ relation change follows from the distinction between those argument classes which can take either the SUBJ or the OBJ function and those which can only take the SUBJ function.

3.1. Semantically Restricted and Unrestricted Functions

The theory of argument classification is based on the distinction between semantically restricted and semantically unrestricted grammatical functions (Bresnan 1982c). The semantically unrestricted functions are SUBJ, OBJ, and OBJ2 and the semantically restricted functions are the oblique functions (e.g. OBL_{goal}, OBL_{agent}, etc.). Semantically restricted functions each identify a particular thematic role while semantically unrestricted functions are not associated with any particular thematic role.

There are four major differences in the syntactic behavior of semantically restricted and semantically unrestricted functions. First, the thematic role of a semantically unrestricted function can vary form verb to verb. So, SUBJs and OBJs of different verbs have different thematic roles. And some SUBJs and OBJs have no thematic role at all. (We will return to OBJ2 below.) Of course the thematic role associated with any oblique function is fixed: OBL_{goal} is always a goal, OBL_{agent} is always an agent, and so on.

(111) a. Jill kicked the ball. *SUBJ is agent*
b. The ball rolled away. *SUBJ is theme*
c. Jill received a letter. *SUBJ is goal*
d. Jill owns a car. *SUBJ is location*
e. Jill likes apples. *SUBJ is experiencer*
f. Spiders scare Jill. *SUBJ is stimulus*

(112) a. The baby kicked the ball. *OBJ is patient*
b. The cook melted the butter. *OBJ is theme*
c. The refugees fled the city. *OBJ is source*
d. Spiders scare Susan. *OBJ is experiencer*
e. Susan likes spiders. *OBJ is stimulus*

Rappaport (1983) uses this property of unrestricted functions to explain well known thematic restrictions on nominalizations. She shows that the "subject" and "object" positions of derived nominals do not cover the same range of thematic roles that SUBJs and OBJs of verbs cover and she claims that the reason for this is that derived nominals do not have SUBJs and OBJs. Instead, all of the functions in a derived nominal are semantically restricted.

A second property of semantically unrestricted functions is that relation changing rules can change their thematic roles. So, the SUBJ and OBJ of a given verb can take on different roles as a result of relation changing rules. (Again, we return to OBJ2 below.)

(113) a. The girl handed the baby a toy. *OBJ is goal*
b. The girl handed a toy to the baby. *OBJ is theme*

(114)a. The cook poked a hole in the potato. *OBJ is theme*
   b. The cook poked the potato. *OBJ is patient*
(115)a. The girl handed the baby a toy. *SUBJ is agent*
   b. A toy was handed to the baby. *SUBJ is theme*
   c. The baby was handed a toy. *SUBJ is goal*
   d. There was a toy handed to the baby. *SUBJ is non-thematic*

A third property of semantically unrestricted functions is cross-linguistic variation in the roles that they usually have. For example, in English, OBJ2s are always themes but according to Maling & Zaenen (1983) and Levin & Simpson (1981), OBJ2 in Icelandic can be a theme or a goal. A more striking type of cross linguistic variation is suggested by the Ergativity Hypothesis (Marantz 1984, B. Levin 1983) which says that truly ergative languages assign the SUBJ function to patients and the OBJ function to agents. Jesse Roberts (personal communication) also suggests that OBJs can be agents in Navajo under certain circumstances.

The fourth property of semantically unrestricted functions is that they enter into two control relationships which are not available to semantically restricted functions. First, only semantically unrestricted functions can be anaphorically controlled. Since PRO-drop is treated as a form of anaphoric control in LFG, there can be PRO-drop languages where a SUBJ, OBJ, or OBJ2 can be dropped but oblique functions are not subject to PRO-drop. Malayalam is such a language (Mohanan 1983).

Second, only unrestricted functions can serve as lexically induced functional controllers. Lexically induced functional control figures in raising constructions, in some cases of equi, and in some cases of secondary predication (Bresnan 1982c).

Bresnan (1982c) explains the limited behavior of obliques as a restriction on the values that can be assigned to OBL functions in the lexicon. She claims that OBL functions can be assigned to thematic argument slots but that they cannot be given values via functional equations. Thus they cannot be lexically induced functional controllers because this type of control is determined in the lexicon by a control equation which assigns a value to the controller. In order for an OBL to be a lexically induced functional controller, it would have to appear in an equation like (↑ OBL) = (↑ XCOMP SUBJ). This, however, is not allowed. Similarly, OBLs cannot be anaphorically controlled. This is because anaphorically controlled elements are introduced in the lexical entries of their governing verbs via equations which give them null pronominal values. In order for an oblique to be anaphorically controlled, it would have to appear in an equation like (↑ OBL) = [PRED PRO, U +]. This also is not allowed.

I suggest a slightly different explanation for the restricted control behavior of obliques. Obliques differ from the semantically unrestricted functions in the way that they are encoded in constituent structure. Oblique function names are determined by reference to their CASE feature in the equation ($(\uparrow (\downarrow \text{CASE})) = \downarrow$).[16] I will call this *semantic encoding*. Semantically unrestricted functions, on the other hand, are encoded independently of their case features. The equations which encode them (e.g. ($\uparrow$ SUBJ) = $\downarrow$) may cooccur with equations which assign or constrain a case value (e.g. ($\downarrow$ CASE) = NOM) but the case value is not crucial to the encoding of the function. I will call this *free encoding*. In configurational languages, freely encoded functions are configurationally encoded and semantically encoded functions are non-configurationally encoded. (See Bresnan (1982c) and Mohanan (1982) for definitions of configurational and non-configurational encoding.) In a non-configurational language, freely encoded functions are those that get a function and a case in contrast to those that get a function via their case.

We can explain the restricted control behavior of oblique functions by sticking strictly to the distinction between freely and semantically encoded functions. This requires taking a slightly different definition of *encoding*. I define an encoding of a function as any mention of the function name in a lexical form or any non-constraint equation which mentions the function. I propose that the only allowable encodings for obliques are semantic encodings (i.e. encoding via a CASE feature) and assignments to thematic argument positions. Obliques therefore cannot occur in functional or anaphoric control equations because in those equations, the encoding of OBL functions would be independent of their CASE value.[17]

Another observed fact about obliques is that they cannot be non-thematic. That is, they are always logical arguments of verbs to which they bear the oblique function. This means that there is no raising into oblique functions (Bresnan 1982c, Chomsky 1981) and there are no oblique pleonastic elements. In order for an oblique to be non-thematic, it would have to appear outside of the angle brackets of a lexical form but this is not allowed because it is

---

[16] This equation is often expanded into two equations: ($\uparrow$ OBL$_x$) = $\downarrow$ and ($\downarrow$ CASE) = OBL$_x$.

[17] The prohibition against mentioning OBL function names also *wrongly* prevents them from being constructionally induced functional controllers if constructionally induced functional control resulted from equations of the form ($\uparrow$ G) = ($\downarrow$ SUBJ) which are associated with controlled phrases. In order for the controller to be OBL, G has to be instantiated with some OBL function name. But this will not be possible if OBL function names are not allowed to appear in encodings.

neither a semantic encoding nor a direct assignment to a thematic argument slot.[18]

I have presented two different taxonomies which separate obliques from the other functions: one based on semantic restrictedness versus semantic unrestrictedness and one based on semantic encoding versus free encoding. The two taxonomies make very similar predictions about the behavior of obliques as controllers, controllees, and non-thematic elements. However, the latter distinction (in terms of encoding) clarifies some properties of OBJ2 and OBL_{ag} which are slightly problematic for a taxonomy which is based on semantic restrictedness.

OBJ2 and OBL_{ag} show signs of being both semantically restricted and unrestricted. OBJ2 acts as if it were unrestricted crosslinguistically by taking different thematic roles in different languages. But in many languages, OBJ2 seems to be semantically restricted because it takes only one or two roles. (For example, in English, all OBJ2s are themes or patients.) OBL_{ag} acts as if it were unrestricted in that it seems to take many different roles (but see Section 2.1) but it seems to be semantically restricted in that it cannot be a lexically induced functional controller.

These functions are not anomalous at all in a taxonomy based on semantic encoding. OBJ2 is freely encoded and OBL_{ag} is semantically encoded. The apparent semantic restrictedness of OBJ2 and the apparent semantic unrestrictedness of OBL_{ag} are not relevant to this distinction. In Section 3.3 I suggest that semantic restrictedness is a property of argument classes while semantic encoding is a property of grammatical functions.

3.2. Argument Classes

This section describes a notion of Argument Classification which plays a prominent role in the theory of relation changing rules. Argument Classification (AC) manages the interaction between semantically conditioned and syntactically productive relation changes. It applies before the assignment of grammatical functions, putting each argument in a lexical form into one of four classes: semantically restricted, subjective unrestricted, general unrestricted, and unexpressed. The argument class severely limits the grammatical function that an argument will have and, in many cases, uniquely determines it.

---

[18] I am assuming, following Wasow, Sag, & Nunberg, that idiom chunks are, in fact, arguments of verbs rather than being non-thematic. Because of the nature of semantically encoded functions proposed here, the treatment of idiom chunks found in Bresnan (1982a) is not allowable. In Bresnan (1982a), idiom chunks were non-thematic but this would preclude the existence of oblique idiom chunks.

The four argument classes are defined in terms of the types of grammatical functions they can take. Arguments in the semantically restricted class must take the semantically restricted functions which match their thematic roles or take no function at all. For example, goals in the semantically restricted class must take the OBL_{goal} function or no function, agents in the semantically restricted class must take the OBL_{agent} function or no function, and so on. Allowing semantically restricted arguments not to take a function reflects the generalization (pointed out to me by Joan Bresnan) that, in general, oblique functions do not have to be expressed.[19]

Subjective unrestricted arguments and general unrestricted arguments may take semantically unrestricted functions but subjective unrestricted arguments can only take the SUBJ function and general unrestricted arguments can take any semantically unrestricted function. And finally, arguments in the unexpressed class do not take any grammatical function at all.

(116)

Class	Function Assignments
subjective unrestricted	SUBJ
general unrestricted	SUBJ, OBJ, OBJ2
semantically restricted	OBL, no function
unexpressed	no function

I will use annotations on predicate argument structure to identify argument classes. A single underline will mark a subjective unrestricted argument; boldface will mark a semantically restricted argument; and Ø will mark an unexpressed argument. General unrestricted functions are not marked. I will not discuss the functions COMP and XCOMP or the argument classes of that they correspond to but I will use italics to mark arguments which take one of the complement functions. The following are examples of lexical forms with classified arguments.

(117)a.　　kick< <u>agent</u>　patient >
　　　　　　　　SUBJ　　OBJ
　　　　　　"The child kicked the ball."

---

[19]Some exceptions to this generalization are *hand* and *put* which do not permit their oblique arguments to be omitted: *The librarian handed a book, *The librarian put a book.

b. kick⟨ <u>agent</u>   patient ⟩
      SUBJ   ∅
   "The child kicked."

c. kick⟨ **agent**   patient ⟩
      OBL$_{ag}$ SUBJ
   "The ball was kicked by the child."

d. kick⟨ **agent**   patient ⟩
      ∅   SUBJ
   "The ball was kicked."

e. occur⟨ theme ⟩
      SUBJ
   "Such things should never occur."

f. work⟨ <u>agent</u> ⟩
      SUBJ
   "Everyone works hard."

g. seem⟨. *theme*   **goal** ⟩ SUBJ
      XCOMP   OBL$_{goal}$
   (↑ SUBJ) = (↑ XCOMP SUBJ)
   "Everyone seems to me to work hard."

h. exist⟨ theme ⟩SUBJ
      OBJ
   (↑ SUBJ) = [U −, LOC +]
   (↑ SUBJ NUM) = (↑ OBJ NUM)
   (↑ SUBJ PERSON) = (↑ OBJ PERSON)
   "There exist many problems."

i. hand⟨ <u>agent</u> theme **goal** ⟩
      SUBJ OBJ   OBL$_{goal}$
   "The girl handed a toy to the baby."

j. hand⟨ <u>agent</u> theme goal ⟩
      SUBJ OBJ2 OBJ
   "The girl handed the baby a toy."

3.3. Another View of Argument Classes

In the previous section I described argument classification in terms of Bresnan's distinction between semantically restricted and semantically unrestricted grammatical functions. In this section, I present an alternative view of argument classification in terms of the distinction between semantically and freely encoded grammatical functions.

In the previous section, a semantically unrestricted argument class was defined as one whose members could be assigned semantically unrestricted functions. However, we could also think of the argument classes themselves as semantically restricted or semantically unrestricted. The semantically unrestricted argument classes would be those whose members could have many different thematic roles. And the semantically restricted classes would be those whose members all had the same thematic role.

As before, there are two semantically unrestricted classes: general unrestricted and subjective unrestricted. The two semantically unrestricted classes differ in *grammatical* restrictedness. The subjective unrestricted class is *grammatically restricted* and can only take the SUBJ function while the general unrestricted class is grammatically unrestricted and can take any function which the Restrictedness Constraint (118) allows.

From this point of view there are several semantically restricted argument classes, one for each thematic role. The semantically restricted goal class contains only goals, the semantically restricted source class contains only sources, and so on.

In the previous section, argument classes were defined in terms of the grammatical functions they could take. Here, argument classes are defined in terms of semantic restrictedness and grammatical restrictedness. The Restrictedness Constraint (118) determines which grammatical functions they can take.

(118)   **Restrictedness Constraint:** Semantically encoded grammatical functions may only be assigned to semantically restricted arguments and freely encoded grammatical functions may only be assigned to semantically unrestricted arguments.

The effect of the Restrictedness Constraint is that only the function assignments in table (116) are allowable. Arguments in the semantically restricted classes can only be oblique because only the OBL functions are semantically encoded. Arguments in the general unrestricted class can be SUBJs, OBJs, or OBJ2s because these are the freely encoded functions. The Restrictedness Constraint would allow arguments in the subjective unrestricted class to take any freely encoded function also, but, as mentioned above, an additional grammatical constraint prevents them from being anything but SUBJs.

Bresnan's semantically unrestricted functions were defined as those that were not inherently associated with any particular thematic role. Some of their defining characteristics were that they could take different roles for different verbs, they could take different roles for the same verb as a result of relation changes, and they could be non-thematic. These characteristics of SUBJ, OBJ and OBJ2 still hold when we think of them as freely encoded functions, but but only the last is a defining characteristic of those functions. The first two characteristics are derived from the interaction of freely encoded functions with semantically unrestricted argument classes.

The freely encoded functions, SUBJ, OBJ, and OBJ2, can take many different thematic roles because they are assigned to semantically unrestricted argument classes which, by definition, can include many different thematic roles. Relation changing rules can change the thematic role of a freely encoded function by assigning the same freely encoded function to a different semantically unrestricted argument. Finally, the ability to be non-thematic follows from the definition of freely encoded functions. Freely encoded functions can appear in any type of encoding, including the non-thematic position outside the angle brackets of a lexical form.

This section and the previous one have presented two different but equivalent definitions of argument classes. Either grammatical functions are defined in terms of semantic restrictedness and argument classes are defined in terms of the functions they can take or grammatical functions are defined in terms of semantic versus free encoding and argument classes are defined in terms semantic restrictedness. I have a slight preference for the latter view for two reasons. The distinction between free and semantic encoding explains properties of OBJ2 and OBL_{ag} which are otherwise problematic (see Section 3.2) and, in conjunction with the Restrictedness Constraint, it explains rather than stipulates the set of allowable grammatical function assignments.

3.4. Two Types of Relation Changing Rules

The distinctions I have discussed suggest a way to separate syntactically productive from semantically conditioned operations. The former I call *purely syntactic rules*, the latter *thematic rules*. In general, the thematic rules change predicate argument structure and argument classifications (ACs) while the purely syntactic rules change the assignment of GFs to classified arguments but we will see that thematic rules may also alter function assignments occasionally.

The division of rules into two types is not new. Similar divisions are proposed by Wasow (1977, 1980) and are discussed by Anderson (1977). Thematic Rules correspond to Wasow's (1980) minor lexical rules and purely syntactic rules (which map ACs onto GFs) correspond to his major lexical rules. The distinction between rule types survives in GB as a distinction between lexical and transformational (non-lexical) rules and it appears in Marantz (1984) as a distinction between rules that alter logico-semantic structure and processes that map logico-semantic structure onto syntactic structure.

Certain properties which distinguish the two types or rules can be extracted from the references cited above. In the following list, I summarize these distinguishing properties.[20]

1. Thematic rules, although they apply to syntactic representations, are defined over semantic classes of verbs (Anderson 1977, Wasow 1980).

2. Thematic rules have exceptions and subregularities even within their semantic domain of application (Wasow 1977, 1980).[21]

3. In terms of traditional rule ordering systems, thematic rules seem to come early in the derivation of a sentence. In particular, many of them seem to apply before passivization and raising. That is, passivization and raising apply to the output of thematic rules. The reason for this in the theory of AC is that the OBJ-to-SUBJ relation change in passivization is the result of purely syntactic rules, as is the assignment of a non-thematic SUBJ or OBJ as controller of an XCOMP (which constitutes raising). Changes in ACs carried out by thematic rules feed these purely syntactic rules by changing the potential for certain arguments to be SUBJs and OBJs. Analogously, Wasow (1977) points out that lexical rules precede transformational rules.

4. Some thematic rules produce relation changes which are not allowable as purely syntactic relation changes. (Recall that the set of possible purely syntactic relation changes is a subset of the set of semantically conditioned relation changes.) The analogous statement in GB is that lexical rules are necessary to account for apparent violations of the projection principle (see also Marantz (1984)).

In LFG with AC there is no clear distinction between rules that assign grammatical relations and those that change them. Arguments appear to undergo relation changes when they can be assigned either of two grammatical relations; thus the theory of relation changes is assimilated to the theory of relation assignments, or to the theory of *grammaticalization*. The two types of relation changing rule correspond to two steps in the assignment of grammatical relations.

---

[20] In addition, Wasow (1977) states that only lexical rules (= thematic rules here) can change the grammatical category of a lexical item, that lexical rules are structure preserving (while transformational rules may not be), and that lexical rules are local (while transformational rules may not be). The latter two criteria are properties of all relation changing rules in LFG with argument classification. The first criterion refers to rules of derivational morphology. These are considered to be thematic rules in two-level LFG, though they are not discussed here in detail.

[21] Of course, in a more refined semantic system, it could turn out that things which seem to be exceptions now are really not exceptions.

The two subsections which follow describe the process of assigning grammatical relations in LFG with AC. Section 3.4.1 deals with classification rules which assign arguments to argument classes based on thematic roles and semantic classes. Classification rules are one type of thematic rule. Other types of thematic rules are discussed in Chapters 4 and 5. Section 3.4.2 deals with purely syntactic rules which apply to the output of the thematic rule component and assign grammatical functions to classified arguments and non-thematic elements.

3.4.1. Classification of Thematic Arguments

A theory of grammaticalization should attempt to define a mapping from the semantic representation of a verb and its arguments to a set of syntactic frames in which the verb can appear. Ideally, many of these frames would be predictable from the semantic representation and would not have to be listed explicitly for each individual verb. This was the point of much research in Case Grammar and Lexical Semantics (Fillmore 1968, Gruber 1976, Jackendoff 1972, 1976, 1984, Hale & Laughren 1983, and Guerssel et al. 1985).

Following Jackendoff (1976) and Hale & Laughren (1983), I assume that verbs are grouped into semantic classes (like Jackendoff's GO, BE, CAUSE, LET, and STAY classes) and that arguments of verbs are grouped according to their thematic roles. Thematic role assignments cut across semantic classes. For example, all semantic classes can have an argument with the theme role, but for a GO verb, the theme is the argument which changes location, possession, or state while for a BE verb, the theme is the argument whose location is predicated.

Generalizations about the grammaticalization of arguments can depend on thematic roles, semantic classes, or both. And, of course, as pointed out in Chapter 2, some generalizations about grammaticalization are syntactically predictable without taking thematic roles or semantic classes into account. Generalizations of the former sort are predicted by the *thematic rule component* of the grammar; generalizations of the latter sort are explained by the *purely syntactic* rule component.

In the system I propose here there are two steps in the assignment of grammatical relations. First, the thematic rule component will contain a set of classification rules, which assign arguments to argument classes. This process is sensitive to the thematic role of the argument and the semantic class of the verb. Next, the purely syntactic rule component assigns grammatical functions to classified arguments. Syntactically productive relation changes are the result of alternate grammatical function assignments.

(119) lists a few classification rules for English which produce the partially specified lexical forms in ((120) a-(120) d). Each rule assigns an argument to an argument class. Notice that ((120) b) differs from the other lexical forms in that it does not have a subjective unrestricted argument. In the theory of AC, the lack of a subjective unrestricted argument is the defining characteristic of an unaccusative verb. The verb *work* is an unergative verb. That is, it is an intrans verb with a subjective unrestricted argument.

(119)   Some Grammaticalization Rules for English

        1. Agent is subjective unrestricted.

        2. Theme is general unrestricted.

        3. Goal is semantically restricted.

        4. Patient is general unrestricted.

(120) a.   'kick< <u>agent</u> patient >'

    b.   'occur< theme >'

    c.   'work< <u>agent</u> >'

    d.   'hand< <u>agent</u> theme **goal** >

The rules in (119) are stated so that they apply to all agents, themes, goals, and patients in all semantic classes of verbs, but as we will see in Chapter 4, there are grammaticalization rules which apply selectively. For example, the Dative Rule assigns goals to the general unrestricted class but it only applies to verbs that express a change of possession or an exchange of information. The dative rule exists along with the rule which assigns goals to the semantically restricted class.

Relation changes appear to take place when two classification rules are applicable to the same argument. For example, since *hand* is a change of possession verb, its goal can either be in the semantically restricted class (by the general classification rule for goals) or in the general unrestricted class (by the Dative Rule). The classification rules therefore produce two partial lexical forms for *hand* ((120) d) and (121).

(121)   'hand< <u>agent</u> theme goal >

Since the goal in ((120) d) is semantically restricted, it will have to take the OBL_{goal} function. And since the goal in (121) is general unrestricted, it will have to take a semantically unrestricted grammatical function — OBJ, in this case. Thus, the goal argument of *hand* will appear to undergo an OBJ/OBL$_{goal}$ relation change.

As this example shows, classification rules are not in an elsewhere-type relationship with each other. Instead, all rules apply when they are applicable.

I will not provide an explicit set of classification rules here, but a few comments are in order. First, thematic rules are essentially language-particular, although some of them are fairly pervasive in the world's languages. This implies rejection of RG's universal alignment hypothesis (that initial grammatical relations are totally predictable from thematic roles and that the rules that assign initial grammatical relations to thematic roles are the same in all languages)[22] in favor of a view where variation in grammaticalization is expected and it is possible to establish a typology of languages based on their grammaticalization rules.[23]

I also reject the little alignment hypothesis (suggested and rejected in Rosen (1982)) which says that, within any one language, the grammatical relations of a verb's arguments are totally determined by the semantic class of the verb and the thematic roles of its arguments. In the system assumed here, argument classes are usually, though not always, predictable in a given language. This reflects Wasow's (1977) observation that lexical rules tend to have idiosyncratic exceptions. I assume that any exceptions to a classification rule are written into the rule. For example, the Dative Rule mentioned above will list the verb *explain* as an exception because its goal is always semantically restricted. However, for the sake of brevity, I will not attempt to list all idiosyncratic exceptions in the formulation of classification rules.

3.4.2. Purely Syntactic Rules

Purely syntactic rules assign grammatical functions to classified arguments. We can assume that functions are assigned freely provided that certain well-formedness conditions are met:

---

[22] This hypothesis is discussed and rejected in Rosen (1982).

[23] See, for example, the Ergativity Hypothesis of Marantz (1984) and B. Levin (1983).

(122) **Well-formedness Conditions on Grammatical Function Assignment**

1. Arguments in the semantically restricted class must have semantically encoded functions.

2. Subjective unrestricted arguments must have the SUBJ function.

3. General unrestricted arguments must have a freely encoded function.

4. Semantically restricted functions cannot be non-thematic.

5. Every argument which is not in the Ø class or the semantically restricted class must get a grammatical function.

6. Each lexical form must have a SUBJ.[24]

7. **Function Argument Biuniqueness:** (Bresnan 1982b) Each function is assigned to at most one argument and each argument gets at most one grammatical function.

The effect of the first four conditions in (122) is that only the grammatical function assignments in (123) are possible. Rules (6)-(8) in (123) may be instantiated more precisely as language-particular rules for assigning certain dummy elements or as universal rules like the Lexical Rule of Functional Control (Bresnan 1982c) discussed in the next section.

(123) **Possible Purely Syntactic Rules**

1. A subjective unrestricted argument is SUBJ.

2. A general unrestricted argument is OBJ.

3. A general unrestricted argument is OBJ2.

4. A general unrestricted argument is SUBJ.

5. A semantically restricted argument is OBL.

6. SUBJ has some non-thematic value.

7. OBJ has some non-thematic value.

8. OBJ2 has some non-thematic value.

---

[24] In the GB framework, Rothstein (1983) proposes that this requirement follows from a general notion of predication. This analysis might also be applicable in LFG.

The last three conditions in (122) further restrict the possible function assignments for a given lexical form. For example, the theme in ((120) b), repeated here, is a general unrestricted argument. So, according to condition (3) in (122) it could be a SUBJ, OBJ, or OBJ2. However, if it were anything other than SUBJ, the resulting lexical form would violate condition (6). Therefore, in order to satisfy condition (6), the theme must be a SUBJ.

(124)a. 'occur< theme >' *output of thematic rules*

b. * 'occur< theme >' *violation of condition (6)*
         OBJ

c. 'occur< theme >' *well-formed GF assignment*
         SUBJ

However, there is another conceivable outcome for ((120) b). The theme could be an OBJ (or OBJ2 — but see below) if the SUBJ function were assigned to some non-thematic dummy value. I pointed out in Chapter 2 that individual languages need not instantiate each of the allowable syntactically productive function assignments and that any allowable syntactically productive operation could occur as a semantically conditioned operation. In English, assignment of dummy values to SUBJ is apparently a semantically conditioned operation which is carried out in the thematic rule component. This means that if an English verb has a dummy SUBJ, that dummy value is specified before the syntactically productive function assignments take place. ((120) b) was meant to represent the lexical form of *occur* at the end of the thematic rule component when it is too late to get a dummy value for SUBJ. Of course, the thematic rule component could produce an alternate form of the same verb with a dummy assignment for SUBJ, ((125) a). The equation ($\uparrow$ SUBJ) = [LOC +, U −] indicates that the SUBJ of *occur* will be the dummy element *there*.

(125)a. 'occur< theme >' *output of thematic rules*

$(\uparrow \text{SUBJ}) = \begin{bmatrix} \text{LOC} & + \\ \text{U} & - \end{bmatrix}$

b. 'occur< theme >' *well-formed GF assignment*
         OBJ

$(\uparrow \text{SUBJ}) = \begin{bmatrix} \text{LOC} & + \\ \text{U} & - \end{bmatrix}$

Italian apparently has a syntactically productive rule for assigning null dummy subjects (Burzio 1981, Baker 1983). So, in that language, the purely syntactic rule component could do one of two things with a form like ((120) b). It could assign SUBJ to theme or it could give SUBJ a dummy value and assign OBJ to theme.

Now consider another example of grammatical function assignment to classified arguments. The patient in ((120) a) is a general unrestricted argument. So, according to condition (3) in (122) it could be a SUBJ, OBJ, or OBJ2. However, the agent argument of the same verb is subjective unrestricted and, therefore, can only be a SUBJ. If the patient took the SUBJ function, then either the agent would also take the SUBJ function and condition (7) would be violated or the agent would not take the SUBJ function and condition (2) would be violated. So, our principles tell us that the patient must be either an OBJ or an OBJ2. So far, there is no well-formedness condition that forces the patient to be an OBJ instead of an OBJ2. But the raising-to-object construction (Section 3.5) provides some insight into how to resolve this choice.

Recall that in LFG with AC, there is no clear distinction between rules that assign grammatical relations and rules that change them. Syntactically productive relation changes occur when an argument alternately takes two different functions without changing its argument class or when a function is alternately assigned to two different values. ((124) c) and ((125) b), for example, represent a syntactically productive SUBJ/OBJ relation change for the theme argument of *occur*. Since this argument is in the general unrestricted class, it can take either the SUBJ or the OBJ function depending on what the circumstances allow. ((126) a) and ((126) b), to take another example, show two lexical forms for the Italian verb *arrivare* (arrive). These forms illustrate two syntactically productive relation changes. First, the theme alternates between SUBJ and OBJ and, second, SUBJ alternates between being thematic and being an unexpressed dummy pronoun. (See Burzio (1981) for evidence that the theme in ((126) b) is an object and not a subject.)

(126)a.   'arrivare< theme >'
                     SUBJ

           Giovanni arriva.
           "G. arrives."

     b.   'arrivare< theme >'
                     OBJ
           (↑ SUBJ) = U   —
                     LOC   —

           Arriva Giovanni.
           "G. arrives."

The conditions in (122) allow very few syntactically productive relation changes. Subjective unrestricted arguments and semantically restricted arguments by definition cannot undergo syntactically productive relation changes because their function is uniquely determined by their argument class. General unrestricted arguments, on the other hand, may take any freely encoded function and therefore can undergo three syntactically productive relation changes: SUBJ/OBJ, SUBJ/OBJ2, and OBJ/OBJ2. In addition, the three freely encoded functions can productively alternate between taking thematic and non-thematic values. Notice that all allowable syntactically productive relation changes involve assignments of freely encoded functions. Any other relation changes must result from changes in the thematic rule component.

3.5. Raising to Object and Transitivity

Control by non-thematic objects (traditionally known as Raising to Object) provides insight into an aspect of lexical representations which has remained vague so far. I described purely syntactic rules as rules which assign grammatical functions, but said nothing about where the grammatical functions come from. One possibility is that they are totally predictable from the output of the thematic rule component and they are chosen as they are needed from a general inventory. Another possibility is that verbs are subcategorized for functions all along and the purely syntactic rules simply take function names from the verb's own subcategorization list and attach them where appropriate.

(127) illustrates these two main possibilities for GF selection. ((127) a) and ((127) b) both show lexical forms before GF assignment. In ((127) a) there are no GFs; They will be chosen as required to satisfy the various well-formedness conditions on lexical forms. In ((127) b), the verb has specified which GFs it will eventually have, but they are not assigned. (Of course, all verbs will have to select GFs which can map onto their classified arguments in a well-formed way.)

(127)a. < _agent_ theme goal >

b. < _agent_ theme goal > SUBJ
OBJ
OBL$_\theta$

A third possibility is that verbs are subcategorized for some functions and not others. Assuming for the moment that this might be the case, I will consider the functions individually. I will conclude that verbs need to be subcategorized for a particular function if some occurences of that function are not predictable from well-formedness conditions and, at the same time, are not random.

Since all lexical forms are required to have SUBJs, all occurrences of SUBJ are predictable from condition (6) in (122). Therefore, it makes little difference where the obligatoriness is expressed. Either all verbs are obligatorily subcategorized for SUBJ or verbs are not subcategorized for SUBJ and it is obligatory to apply a purely syntactic rule which introduces SUBJ.

Similar reasoning applies to the oblique functions. It is always possible to have an OBL_θ function when the matching semantically restricted argument is present. Furthermore, since OBL_θ functions attach only to matching semantically restricted arguments, there cannot be a situation where a verb would idiosyncratically select an oblique function in the absence of a semantically restricted argument class. In other words, all occurrences of OBL_θ are predictable from a well-formedness condition. So again, it makes little difference whether verbs that have semantically restricted arguments are obligatorily subcategorized for the corresponding oblique or whether it is obligatory that some rule applies which introduces an oblique function.

However, the method of function selection *could* make a difference for the OBJ function. Since OBJ is not obligatory in all lexical forms and since it can show up as non-thematic, there could be occurrences of OBJ which are not predictable from a well-formedness condition. However since these "unpredictable" objects do not occur with all verbs, the verbs that do take them must be individually subcategorized for them.

Raising-to-object sentences contain these "unpredictable" objects and, therefore, provide evidence that verbs are subcategorized for the object function. In order to see this, consider the lexical form for *consider* (as in *We consider him happy*) without the introduction of a non-thematic object, ((128) a). Although I will not discuss the functions which are clause nuclei (COMP and XCOMP), I will assume that they have an argument class of their own which I will call comp. Comps are italicized.

(128)a.   'consider< <u>considerer</u>   *considered* >'
                          SUBJ   XCOMP

    b.   'consider< <u>considerer</u>   *considered* >OBJ'
                          SUBJ   XCOMP
               (↑ OBJ) = (↑ XCOMP SUBJ)

((128) a) cannot be complete as it is because the XCOMP does not have a controller. If the XCOMP does not get a controller, then it will be incomplete in f-structure because it will not have a SUBJ. In theory, the SUBJ of *consider* could be the controller, so OBJ does not *have to* be introduced in order to save the form from ill-formedness. Nevertheless, OBJ *is* introduced as the controller ((128) b).

The non-thematic object in ((128) b) cannot be introduced by a purely syntactic rule because OBJ is not *always* introduced in situations similar to ((128) a). Equi verbs with subject controllers look identical to ((128) a) before introduction of the control equation (as in ((129) a)), but non-thematic objects are not assigned to them. Because of this, raising-to-object verbs must distinguish themselves from subject-equi verbs by explicitly selecting an object.

(129) a.   'try< <u>tryer</u>   *tried* >'
                 SUBJ   XCOMP

    b.   'try< <u>tryer</u>   *tried* >'
                 SUBJ   XCOMP
            (↑ SUBJ) = (↑ XCOMP SUBJ)

Given that raising-to-object verbs must be explicitly subcategorized for OBJ, the next question to ask is whether all verbs that take objects select them or whether all remaining OBJs (aside from the OBJs of raising-to-object verbs) are introduced as they are needed by purely syntactic rules.

Competition between OBJ and OBJ2 for general unrestricted arguments argues in favor of explicit subcategorization for OBJ. If verbs did not select OBJ explicitly, some hierarchical principle would have to be called upon in order to determine that, when there is a general unrestricted argument, it is an OBJ and not an OBJ2. The lexical default expressed in (130) captures (but does not really explain) the distribution of OBJ and OBJ2. If a lexical form contains a subjective unrestricted argument and a general unrestricted argument, then (130) determines that it will have an OBJ. If it only has one general unrestricted argument, then it cannot also have an OBJ2 (unless the OBJ2 is non-thematic) because there would be no argument that the OBJ2 could legally attach to. The only situation where there will be an OBJ and OBJ2 is when there are two general unrestricted arguments.

(130)   Lexical Default: Lexical forms that contain both a subjective unrestricted argument and a general unrestricted argument are subcategorized for the OBJ function.

I will represent subcategorization for OBJ by placing the OBJ function outside of the quotation marks that delimit a lexical form. This indicates that it has not yet been assigned. ((131) a) shows the verb *consider* at the end of the thematic rule component before any GF assignments have taken place. ((131) b) shows the verb *kick* at the end of the thematic rule component before any GF assignments. Verbs that select OBJ are *transitive* and verbs that do not select OBJ are *intransitive*.

(131) a.   'consider< <u>considerer</u>   *considered* >'   OBJ

b.   'kick< <u>agent</u>   patient >'   OBJ

After GF assignment, OBJ will appear inside the quote marks, either attached to a general unrestricted argument (as in ((132) a)) or outside the angle brackets as a non-thematic function (as in ((128) b)). Forms schematized in ((132) b) where the OBJ function does not eventually get assigned are ill-formed.

(132) a.   'see< <u>agent</u>   patient >'
                     SUBJ   OBJ

b.   * '<.......>'   OBJ

Assuming subcategorization for OBJ, (133), rather than ((128) a) is the correct form for *consider* at the point where all functions except OBJ have been assigned.

(133)   'consider< <u>considerer</u>   *considered* >'   OBJ
                          SUBJ   XCOMP

An advantage of (133) over ((128) a) is that it allows the Lexical Rule of Functional Control (Bresnan 1982c) to apply uniformly to raising and equi verbs. The lexical rule of functional control applies to forms with XCOMPs and predicts the GF of the controller based on the verb's inventory of subcategorized functions. The Lexical Rule of Functional Control is a purely syntactic rule which assigns non-thematic values to freely encoded functions.

(134)   **Lexical Rule of Functional Control:**

Let L be a lexical form, and let F_L be the grammatical function assignment of L. If XCOMP ϵ F_L, then add to L the equation

($\uparrow$ OBJ2) = ($\uparrow$ XCOMP SUBJ) if OBJ2 ϵ F_L

otherwise

($\uparrow$ OBJ) = ($\uparrow$ XCOMP SUBJ) if OBJ ϵ F_L

otherwise

($\uparrow$ SUBJ) = ($\uparrow$ XCOMP SUBJ)

3.6. Properties of Relation Changing Rules

In Chapters 4 and 5 I will apply the theory of argument classification to a number of rules in English and Dutch. To close this chapter, I will briefly explain how the theory of argument classification accounts for the properties of relation changing rules which were listed in Chapter 2.

The theory of argument classification allows the SUBJ function to be assigned to a subjective unrestricted argument, to a general unrestricted argument, or to a non-thematic value. Thus, in effect, there are three types of SUBJ. URs are rules that distinguish subjective unrestriced SUBJs from one or both of the other types of SUBJ. URs separate active transitive verbs from passive verbs because the former always have subjective unrestricted SUBJs while the latter always have general unrestricted subjects. Furthermore, intransitive verbs fall into two classes depending on whether their SUBJs are subjective unrestricted or general unrestricted. Finally, some URs treat OBJs like passive subjects because both are in the general unrestricted argument class. In other words, URs are sensitive to argument classifications instead of (or in addition to) grammatical functions.

The theory of argument classification also explains the apparent directionality of the SUBJ/OBJ relation change. General unrestricted arguments take either the SUBJ or the OBJ function depending on whether there is another SUBJ in the lexical form. Thus, general unrestricted arguments (and certain non-thematic elements such as raised objects) are OBJs in some sentences but can be SUBJs in some related sentences. Subjective unrestricted arguments correspond to what I called canonical subjects in Chapter 2. They can only take the SUBJ function and never show up as OBJs in any related sentences.

The thematic rule component in the theory of argument classification produces semantically conditioned relation changes. As we will see in the next chapter, thematic rules can add/delete arguments with particular thematic roles to/from verbs of particular semantic classes. For example, the causative/inchoative rule adds/deletes the agent argument of agent-theme verbs. Thematic rules also perform special argument class assignments for verbs in certain semantic classes. For example, the Dative Rule (Chapter 4) assigns goals of change of possession verbs to the general unrestricted argument class. Because of the restrictiveness of the well-formedness conditions in (122), a change in argument class will, in general, force a change in grammatical function assignment. These changes in grammatical function assignment will appear to be semantically conditioned because the change in argument class that triggered them is semantically conditioned. Thematic rules can also perform special-case grammatical function assignments directly.

Syntactic productivity is a property of the purely syntactic rule component where grammatical function assignments are made without regard to thematic roles or semantic classes. Syntactically productive operations are predictable from semantically conditioned operations because, given a list of classified arguments, the well-formedness conditions in (122) allow little or no choice of grammatical function assignments. Any change in argument classification will produce a predictable change in grammatical functions.

Notice that the only possible syntactically productive operations involve assignments of semantically unrestricted functions. SUBJ, OBJ, and OBJ2 can alternate between thematic and non-thematic values and general unrestricted arguments can alternate between being SUBJ, OBJ, or OBJ2. Any alternation of a semantically restricted function with an unrestricted one (e.g. an OBJ/OBL relation change or a SUBJ/OBL relation change) must be the result of a reclassification in the thematic rule component. If no reclassification occurred, then there would have to be a violation of the well-formedness conditions because there is no argument class which can take both unrestricted and restricted grammatical functions.

Chapter 4
Formulation of Rules: English

This chapter and the next one illustrate the theory of AC with examples from English and Dutch. In particular, they illustrate the interaction of semantic conditioning with syntactic productivity, the treatment of unaccusative rules, and the apparent directionality of the SUBJ/OBJ relation change.

The rules which I formulate in this chapter raise three additional issues. First, all of the rules bear on the status of Burzio's Generalization (Burzio 1981). I formulate a near equivalent of Burzio's Generalization in the theory of AC and take it to represent the unmarked cases of transitivity. The generalization itself is not given as an axiom. Rather, it is derivable from the requirement that lexical forms of verbs have subjects. (Massam (1984) makes a similar point in GB.) Marked cases of transitivity arise in the presence of certain marked types of subjects.

Second, my treatment of the Dative Object construction embodies claims about the representation of grammatical relations which are substantially different from those made by Relational Grammar, Marantz (1984), or Government and Binding Theory. While in many cases, my general unrestricted arguments are analogous to deep objects, initial objects and logico-semantic objects, they do not have an analogous status in the theory. Some puzzling properties of double object constructions are the existence of two noun phrases whose syntactic behavior is partly the same and partly different and the fact that in some languages they are more the same while in other languages they are more different. The sameness, in the theory of AC, comes from the fact that they are both general unrestricted arguments. An analogous treatment of double objects in other theories would involve some loss of generalization about uniqueness of grammatical relations or the one-to-one pairing of case assigners and case assignees. But the non-uniqueness of the general unrestricted class is built into the theory of AC. Furthermore, the theory predicts the existence of other constructions which contain two general unrestricted arguments and I believe that these constructions do exist in English and Dutch.

A third issue comes out in the discussion of the Pleonastic *there* construction and the Oblique Inversion construction. These constructions contain sentence-initial phrases which pass some tests for subjecthood and not others. Similar patterns of syntactic behavior in other languages have been used by Perlmutter (1979, 1982) to argue for multi-stratal representations of grammatical relations and the notion of Working 1. (Although I do not know of any analysis of English Oblique Inversion in Relational Grammar, I believe that the LFG treatment of that construction can be compared to RG treatment of inversion constructions.) I claim that pleonastic *There* and fronted obliques in English pass certain tests for subjecthood because they are SUBJs and that they fail other tests because they are pleonastic (in a sense that will become clear). My analysis captures certain similarities in the behavior of dummy subjects and fronted obliques with respect to tests for subjecthood. Furthermore, it correctly predicts which tests they will pass and which tests they will fail with a degree of explanatory adequacy which, I believe, has not been acheived by RG in its treatment of inversion constructions (see also Watanabe (1985)). In Chapter 5, I will show how the analysis extends to an inversion construction in Dutch.

4.1. The Causative/Inchoative Rule

In Chapter 2, the causative/inchoative rule served as an example of a semantically conditioned or thematic rule, and in Chapter 1 it served as an example of a rule that changes predicate argument structure. Here, I will illustrate the formulation of thematic rules and predicate argument structure-changing rules in the theory of AC (Subsection 4.1.1) using the causative/inchoative rule and I will also use the causative/inchoative rule to discuss the treatment of transitivity in the theory of AC (Subsection 4.1.2).

The causative/inchoative rule relates the (a) and (b) sentences below.

(135) a. She turned the pumpkin into a coach.
     b. The pumpkin turned into a coach.
(136) a. The projectionist started the movie.
     b. The movie started.
(137) a. They hung the clothes on the line.
     b. The clothes hung on the line.

4.1.1. Formulation

In LFG with AC, thematic rules have three components: a semantic domain, a body, and a list of exceptions. The semantic domain specifies which verbs the rule applies to in terms of thematic roles and semantic classes. The causative/inchoative rule, as formulated in (138), lists the semantic classes of $GO_{position}$, $GO_{identity}$, and STAY verbs as its semantic domain.

The body of the causative/inchoative rule shows that it is a particular type of thematic rule, namely one that creates new predicate argument structures. In LFG with AC, such rules can be represented as lexical redundancy rules; they express a relationship between two lexical forms which are derived independently from different thematic rules rather than being derived from each other. Lexical redundancy rules in LFG consist of two lexical form schemata separated by a double headed arrow which is interpreted as follows: any verb which has a lexical form matching the schema on the one side of the arrow also has a lexical form matching the schema on the other side. The Agent-Theme Rule states that any $GO_{position}$ or $GO_{identity}$ verb[25] which appears in the lexicon with an agent, a theme, and possibly some other arguments (represented by ellipses) will have an alternate lexical form which differs only in that it lacks an agent argument. (I'm assuming that the ellipses on the right side of the arrow do not contain an agent.) Similarly, a $GO_{position}$ or $GO_{identity}$ verb whose lexical form contains a theme (and possibly some other arguments represented by ellipses) has an alternate form which is identical except for the presence of an agent.[26] The causative/inchoative rule simply reflects the fact that many GO verbs have two lexical forms such as those in ((139) a) and ((139) b).

(138)   The Causative/Inchoative Rule: applies to STAY, $GO_{position}$, and $GO_{identity}$ verbs.

⟨ .... agent   theme .... ⟩ ⟨---⟩ ⟨ .... theme .... ⟩

exceptions: *arrive, die, place, put, tint, demolish, transport....*

(139)a.   'turn⟨ agent   theme   goal ⟩'

"She turned him into a frog."

---

[25] According to Jackendoff's (1976) classification, $GO_{identity}$ verbs express a change of state and $GO_{position}$ verbs express a change of location.

[26] Actually, the most economical formulation of the rule would not have to mention the theme because all GO verbs have themes.

b.   'turn< theme goal >'

"He turned into a frog."

Exceptions to the causative/inchoative rule are verbs that are in the semantic domain of the rule and do not have one of the forms predicted by the rule. These include intransitive GO_{pos} and GO_{ident} verbs (like *arrive* and *die*) which never occur with an agent, as well as transitive GO_{pos} and GO_{ident} verbs (like *tint* and *transport*) which never occur without an agent. The list of exceptions to (138) is quite long, but it could be shortened by refining the semantic domain and the theory of lexical semantics in which it is framed.

The causative/inchoative rule is designed to work modularly with the rest of the thematic rule component. It does not have to mention, change, or assign any argument classes because the normal application of classification rules will produce the correct results independently. For example, after the Agent-Theme Rule determines that *turn* has the two lexical forms in ((139) a) and ((139) b), the classification rules in ((140) a-(140) c) produce the partially specified lexical forms in ((141) a) and ((141) b).

(140)a.   Agent is subjective unrestricted.
b.   Theme is general unrestricted.
c.   Goal is semantically restricted.

(141)a.   'turn< <u>agent</u> theme **goal** >'

"She turned him into a frog."

b.   'turn< theme **goal** >'

"He turned into a frog."

Resultative secondary predication supports the claim that themes of intransitive GO verbs are general unrestricted in English. In Chapter 2, I showed that resultative secondary predicates are controlled by subjects of passives, objects of transitive verbs, and subjects of some intransitive verbs. In terms of AC, resultative secondary predicates are controlled by general unrestricted arguments (Simpson 1983a) Since subjects of intransitive GO verbs can control resultatives (*solid* and *to a crisp* in the following examples), they must be general unrestricted arguments. This is consistent with the claim that the causative/inchoative rule does not affect argument classifications and that ((140) b) is responsible for the classification of the theme argument.

(142)a.   The river froze solid.

b. The cookies burned to a crisp.

4.1.2. The Causative/Inchoative Rule and Transitivity

This subsection addresses the interaction of the causative/inchoative rule with the purely syntactic rule component. It turns out that the causative/inchoative rule ultimately triggers a SUBJ/OBJ relation change and a change in transitivity but neither of these things needs to be specified by the rule itself. Instead, they follow from the normal application of the purely syntactic rules.

In Chapter 2, I argued that verbs had to be idiosyncratically subcategorized for the OBJ function but that, in most cases, the presence or absence of the OBJ function was determined by certain default rules. One such rule is Lexical Default 1, repeated here from Chapter 2, and another is Lexical Default 2.

(143) Lexical Default 1: Lexical forms that contain both a subjective unrestricted argument and a general unrestricted argument are subcategorized for the OBJ function.

(144) Lexical Default 2: Lexical forms that have a general unrestricted argument and no subjective unrestricted argument are optionally subcategorized for the OBJ function.

As a result of the lexical default rules, each verb that undergoes the Agent-Theme Rule will have three partially specified lexical forms like those schematized in ((145) a-(145) c). These forms exist just before grammatical function assignment.

(145) a. '< ... agent theme ... >' OBJ

    b. '< ... theme ... >' OBJ

    c. '< ... theme ... >'

After grammatical function assignment, lexical form ((145) a) will show up as a typical transitive verb like ((146) a) and lexical form ((145) c) will show up as a typical intransitive verb like ((146) b). Notice that ((146) a) and ((146) b) are the only possible well-formed grammatical function assignments for ((145) a) and ((145) c). The OBJ/SUBJ relation change of the theme, therefore, follows from the usual operation of the purely syntactic rules and the lexical default rules for transitivity.

(146) a. '< ... agent theme ... >'
               SUBJ OBJ

b.   '⟨ ... theme ... ⟩'
       SUBJ

Lexical form ((145) b) will have no well-formed GF assignment in English. If SUBJ is assigned to the theme, then the form will be ill-formed because it will not use the OBJ function which it is subcategorized for. On the other hand, if OBJ were assigned to the theme, then the form could be well-formed as long as SUBJ were assigned to some pleonastic value. However, rules which assign pleonastic subjects in English are apparently all semantically constrained and they do not seem to apply to verbs which undergo the Agent-Theme Rule. Therefore, there can be no pleonastic subjects for these verbs and, as a result, their themes cannot be OBJs.

Lexical Default Rule 2, along with the requirement that lexical forms have subjects, captures the often observed generalization that verbs which do not have canonical subjects (going back to the theory-neutral terminology from Chapter 2) tend to be intransitive. In the theory of AC, canonical subjects are subjects that are in the subjective unrestricted class. If there is no subjective unrestricted argument (i.e. no canonical subject), then the SUBJ function must be assigned in some other way. In particular, it can be assigned to a general unrestricted argument. Since verbs typically do not have more than one general unrestricted argument, assigning SUBJ to that argument precludes assigning OBJ anywhere in the lexical form and the result will have to be intransitive.

There are two marked situations in which a verb which lacks a subjective unrestricted argument can take the OBJ function. One has already been discussed: a general unrestricted argument can be an OBJ in the absence of a subjective unrestricted argument provided that the SUBJ function gets some non-thematic value. The other situation arises when a verb has two general unrestricted arguments. In this case, one can take the SUBJ function while the other takes the OBJ function. I claim that this is the case for certain English verbs like *fit* and *suit* which do not passivize and for passives of double object verbs in some languages. I discuss these verbs further in Section 4.2 and in Chapter 5.

Similar facts about transitivity are captured in GB by Burzio's Generalization[27] (147) and the case filter. Burzio's generalization states that verbs assign accusative case[28] if and only if they have thematic subjects.

---

[27] See Burzio (1981), B. Levin (1983), and Massam (1984).

[28] In GB there is a distinction between morphological case and abstract Case. Burzio's Generalization deals with abstract Case.

(147)   T <···> A

If a verb has a thematic subject, then it can assign accusative case and therefore can have an object because this object will be able to receive case. On the other hand, if a verb does not have a thematic subject, then it does not assign accusative case. In this situation, the verb cannot assign case to an object so it will either have to be intransitive or transmit nominative case to its object via co-superscripting with a dummy subject. This accurately reflects the fact that, in many languages, verbs with dummy subjects agree with a nominative NP in object position.

Burzio's generalization does not extend so well to certain cases which I discuss in the next section where, I claim, there are two general unrestricted arguments. In many of these situations, one of the general unrestricted arguments does get accusative case. (Massam (1984 LSA talk) also makes this point.) These are counterexamples to the generalization as stated in (147).

The mistake in Burzio's generalization is its reliance on case to control transitivity. In order to account for the intransitivity of verbs without thematic subjects, Burzio had to claim that they did not assign accusative case. But this fails to account for verbs without thematic subjects which do assign accusative case. In LFG the intransitivity of verbs without subjective unrestricted arguments simply follows from the requirement that lexical forms have subjects. The absence of accusative case marking on objects of verbs with dummy subjects follows from general principles of case assignment and agreement which are independent of the principles controlling transitivity.[29,30]

To conclude the discussion of the causative/inchoative rule, I will simply point out that, as is typical of thematic rules, it appears to feed purely syntactic rules. For example, it feeds constructions where subjects are controlled because it indirectly creates new subjects

---

[29] In particular, I am assuming that verbs assign nominative case in the lexicon to the highest ranking freely encoded function which does not already have a lexically specified quirky case, where SUBJ ranks higher than OBJ. Nominative case is not assigned to non-thematic subjects which do not have person and number features, such as pleonastic *there*, but it is assigned to pleonastics like *it* which do have person and number features. Nominative case is optionally assigned to non-thematic subjects which control an XCOMP in order to accomodate the situations where the controller is pleonastic *there* as well as the situations where the controller is a regular NP with person and number features.

[30] Joan Bresnan points out that there is sometimes accusative case with dummy subjects. One possible example is an English sentence like *There's me and him* and other possible examples occur in French and Welsh. These constitute counterexamples to Burzio's Generalization.

(regardless of whether it creates transitive verbs from intransitive verbs or vice versa) by changing AC and predicate argument structure in a way that forces the purely syntactic rules to change the assignment of SUBJ.[31]

4.2. Double Object Rules

4.2.1. The Representation of Double Object Constructions

Double object constructions (like those in (148)) and rules that produce them present a challenge to syntactic theories. Most theories have some sort of functional uniqueness principle which prevents two phrases from having the same GF in the same clause. So, double object sentences (according to these theories) cannot really have two objects and one of the NPs following the verb must have some other function. The hard problem is to determine what the other function is and what properties it has.

(148)a.   Susan handed her the salt.
     b.   Fred cooked Susan a steak.

In LFG, the "other" function (besides OBJ) is OBJ2. OBJ2 is a freely encoded function and is correctly predicted to share certain syntactic behavior with other freely encoded functions. For example, it can be a lexically induced functional controller and an anaphoric controllee in languages that allow control of non-subjects (Bresnan 1982c). Furthermore, OBJ2 has different roles in different languages and, in some languages, (e.g. Icelandic, according to Maling & Zaenen (1983)) OBJ2 can have different roles in different situations. Thus, LFG differs from other theories where the second object in a double object construction is considered to be some sort of oblique (Marantz 1984) or chômeur.

((149) a) and ((149) b) show the lexical forms for the double object sentences in ((148) a) and ((148) b).

---

[31]Many other properties of inchoatives are discussed by Keyser and Roeper (1984). K&R show that many rules of derivational morphology treat inchoatives (which they call ergatives) differently from middle verbs (*These books sell well*). They conclude that middle verbs are transitive in the lexicon, but that inchoatives undergo move-α in the lexicon so that they are no longer transitive. The most closely analogous statement in terms of AC would be that the theme argument of an inchoative is subjective unrestricted while the theme or patient of a middle is general unrestricted. This is not unreasonable (In fact, as K&R point out, it explains why inchoatives appear in *there*-insertion sentences less often than other non-agentive intransitive verbs.), but it is not what I assume here.

Keyser and Roeper's conclusion depends on the assumption that the morphological rules in question are sensitive to transitivity. Under alternative formulations, the same rules could be made sensitive to the presence/absence of the agent argument which is deleted from inchoatives though not from middles. (Certain differences between middles and passives, which both retain their agent arguments, would still have to be explained.) In any case, K&R's arguments cannot be translated into LFG with ACs without first formulating the relevant rules of derivational morphology, which I am not prepared to do here.

(149)a.   'hand< <u>agent</u>   theme   goal >'
                    SUBJ   OBJ2   OBJ
           "Susan handed her salt."

    b.   'cook< <u>agent</u>   theme   benefactive >'
                   SUBJ   OBJ2   OBJ
           "Fred cooked Susan a steak."

    My analysis of double object constructions depends on allowing one lexical form to have two general unrestricted arguments. Thus, although argument classes in LFG seem to be analogous to deep structure in GB or to initial grammatical relations in RG, they differ from deep or initial grammatical relations in a crucial way: they are not subject to a uniqueness principle. In this section and in Chapter 5, I demonstrate that the non-uniqueness of argument classes leads to an insightful treatment of double object constructions, inversion constructions, and certain unpassivizable predicates.

    Although argument classes are non-unique, the uniqueness of grammatical functions indirectly imposes restrictions on the number of arguments in each class. For example, a lexical form could never contain two subjective unrestricted arguments because there would have to be two SUBJs to accommodate them. On the other hand, functional uniqueness does not prevent the existence of two general unrestricted arguments provided that they have different grammatical functions. For example, one can be an OBJ while the other is an OBJ2 (as shown above) or one could be a SUBJ while the other is an OBJ or an OBJ2. I claim that the second situation holds for certain unpassivizable predicates in English and Dutch.

    In Section 4.4 I propose that passive lexical forms result from a classification rule whose domain of application is largely coextensive with the classification rule which creates subjective unrestricted arguments. The overall effect is that for transitive verbs (with a few exceptions), any argument which can be subjective unrestricted can also be classified as semantically restricted by the passive classification rule. In light of this, a possible explanation for the non-passivizability of certain apparently transitive verbs is that their subjects do not fall in the domain of either the active classification rule for subjective unrestricted arguments or the passive classification rule. The subjects of these verbs could, in fact, be general unrestricted arguments.

    ((150) e) and ((150) f) are possible lexical forms for the verb *suit* in ((150) c) which does not passivize. The other verbs below would have similar lexical representations. Notice that in the theory of AC these qualify as unaccusative verbs because their subjects are general unrestricted arguments, but they differ from other unaccusative verbs in that they take objects. As far as I know, LFG with AC is the only theory which predicts their existence.

(150) a. I have a book.
b. I got a book.
c. That suits you.
d. That dress fits you.

e. 'suit< theme   loc >'
          SUBJ   OBJ

f. 'suit< theme   loc >'
          SUBJ   OBJ2

These forms are counterexamples to Burzio's Generalization (BG). According to BG, verbs without canonical subjects (= thematic subjects or deep subjects in GB) do not assign accusative case to an object. However, the verbs in ((150) a-(150) d) do appear to assign accusative case as evidenced by the pronoun in *The dress suits her/me/him/us*.

BG was intended to account for the syntactic behavior of verbs without canonical subjects. Lack of case on the object explained why it either had to move to subject position or get nominative case transmitted to it from a dummy element in subject position. But if verbs without canonical subjects are allowed to assign accusative case, then there must be some other account for this pattern.

In Section 4.1 I claimed that the behavior of verbs without canonical subjects followed from the condition that sentences need to have subjects. If there is no subjective unrestricted argument, then either a general unrestricted argument or a dummy element must take the SUBJ function. If there are two general unrestricted arguments, one can fill the SUBJ function while the other takes on OBJ or OBJ2.

The approach described in the preceding paragraph does not depend on case and is, therefore, not contradicted by sentences like ((150) a-(150) d). Furthermore, it allows passives of double object verbs which also appear to assign accusative case to a post-verbal NP in spite of the fact that they have no canonical (subjective unrestricted) subject. ((151) a) shows the lexical form for a passive double object sentence. The goal argument takes the SUBJ function because the theme is pre-associated with OBJ2 before grammatical function assignment takes place (see the formulation of the dative rule in (157)).

(151)a.   'give< agent   theme   goal >'
                   OBL$_{ag}$ OBJ2   SUBJ

"She was given a book by her friends."

There is one consequence of BG which I have not yet explained. Many verbs without canonical subjects assign nominative case to an NP object position. These include verbs with dummy subjects and verbs with non-nominative subjects such as the Icelandic verbs in ((152) a) and ((152) b). If, as I claim, absence of a canonical subject is not tied to absence of accusative case, then we need some other way to explain why so many verbs without canonical subjects do not seem to assign accusative case. I assume that the rules for assigning nominative case to an OBJ depend on whether or not the subject is nominative and on whether or not the subject is pleonastic. They do not depend on whether or not the subject is canonical.

(152)a.   'gefinn< agent   theme   goal >'
                    OBL$_{ag}$ OBJ2   SUBJ

Henni (Dat) var   gefinn bíllinn (Nom).
her   was   given   car-the
"She was given the car."

b.   'sýnast< experiencer *theme* > OBJ'
                SUBJ   XCOMP
(↑ OBJ) = (↑ XCOMP SUBJ)

Mér (Dat) sýnist hann (Nom) vera   góður   drengur.[32]
me   seems he   to-be   good   fellow
"He seems to me to be a good fellow."

In summary: I have argued that it is possible for a verb to have two general unrestricted arguments and I have claimed that this provides a simple account of double object sentences as well as an explanation for the unpassivizability of certain apparently transitive verbs. I then demonstrated that, in my analysis, these unpassivizable verbs were counterexamples to Burzio's Generalization because they appear to assign accusative case in spite of the fact that they have no canonical subject. I concluded that the syntactic behavior of verbs without canonical subjects is determined by the requirement that sentences have subjects and not on the absence of accusative case. I also concluded that the absence of accusative case on an object depends on the case and semantic content of the subject, not on its argument class.

---

[32] Andrews 1982, example (50i).

To close this subsection, notice that a sentence could have three general unrestricted arguments if they had the functions SUBJ, OBJ and OBJ2. A possible example is *I'll have me some fun*.

4.2.2. Formulation of Double Object Rules

The Dative Rule and the Benefactive Rule are responsible for the alternation between the (a) and (b) sentences below. ((155) a) and ((155) b) show the lexical forms for the (a) sentences. ((149) a) and ((149) b) show the lexical forms for the (b) sentences. The lexical forms for the (a) and (b) sentences differ in both AC and GF assignments.

(153)a. Susan handed the salt to her.
   b. Susan handed her the salt.

(154)a. Fred cooked a steak for Susan.
   b. Fred cooked Susan a steak.

(155)a. 'hand< agent   theme   goal >'
                SUBJ   OBJ OBL_{goal}

   b.   'cook< agent   theme   ben >'
                SUBJ   OBJ OBL_{ben}

The Dative Rule is formulated in (157) as a thematic rule. Notice that it has three parts: a semantic domain, a body, and a list of exceptions. The body of the Dative Rule is a classification rule for goal arguments which operates on the lexicon along with the less semantically constrained classification rule for goals repeated here as (156) from Chapter 2. Many verbs can use (156) because it is not restricted to a particluar semantic class.[33] However, (157) is restricted to change of possession verbs and verbs of oral or visual transfer (e.g. *show* and *tell*).

(156)   Goal is semantically restricted.

(157)   **Dative Rule:**

   For change of possession verbs and verbs of oral or visual transfer:
   goal is general unrestricted and theme is OBJ2.

   Exceptions: *explain, present* ....

In addition to classifying a goal as general unrestricted, the Dative Rule also pre-

---

[33] Rule (156) is a thematic rule and, technically, should have three parts. However, since the rule is so general, I have not included a statement of semantic domain or exceptions.

associates OBJ2 with a theme argument. The pre-association is necessary because otherwise the purely syntactic rules could legally assign OBJ or OBJ2 to either the theme or the goal. But in American English, only the goal behaves like an OBJ (e.g. it becomes the SUBJ of the corresponding passive) in a double object sentence.

Recall that all classification rules apply whenever they can. Therefore, both (156) and (157) will apply to the change of possession verbs and verbs of oral and visual transfer. When they apply to the predicate argument structures of these verbs, these rules will result in two different lexical forms such as the ones shown in (158). Purely syntactic rules straightforwardly map the ACs in ((158) a) and ((158) b) onto the full lexical forms in ((149) a) and ((155) a).

(158)a.   < agent theme goal >

b.   < agent theme goal >
                   OBJ2

Pre-association of OBJ2 with theme could be a source of dialect difference between British and American English. For example, the passivizability of either NP in a double object sentence in British English could indicate that either one can be an OBJ, which would be possible if the rule did not pre-associate OBJ2 with the theme argument. Icelandic also has double object sentences where either NP can apparently be the OBJ.[34] These are discussed most recently in Zaenen and Maling (1983). See also Andrews (1982) and Levin & Simpson (1981).

The Dative Rule shows something about the interaction of thematic and purely syntactic rules. Assignment of GFs is basically the job of purely syntactic rules. However, thematic rules may carry out a function assignment (such as the pre-association of OBJ2 in this case) provided that it conforms to the well-formedness conditions on lexical forms. The difference between a grammatical function assignment carried out by a purely syntactic rule and one carried out by a thematic rule is that the latter will apply in semantically restricted circumstances while the former will apply whenever the appropriate AC is present and other syntactic conditions are favorable.

---

[34] Allowing theme and goal to take turns being OBJs creates difficulties in the encoding of functions in c-structure because word order does not reflect the relation change. The goal argument always comes first regardless of whether it is an OBJ or an OBJ2. Currently in LFG, order can only be determined by grammatical function and there is no way to enforce the goal-theme order which is independent of function (Zaenen and Maling 1983). Joan Bresnan suggests a possible solution which seems to be much needed in Bantu languages as well as in Icelandic. She proposes to break up the uniformity of the OBJ function and have many different OBJ functions subscripted with their thematic roles (e.g. OBJ_{theme}, OBJ_{goal}). These functions would be freely encoded even though they are semantically restricted, so the theory of purely syntactic rules would not have to be changed. The various object functions could then be ordered according to their thematic roles.

The Dative rule is a typical thematic rule. It applies to semantically defined classes of verbs (Wasow 1980), and it is ridden with lexical exceptions (Halliday 1967). Furthermore, the Dative rule seems to apply before the OBJ-to-SUBJ relation change of passivization. It feeds passivization by creating new general unrestricted arguments which become new OBJs. Finally, the Dative rule appears to violate restrictions on GF assignment in the sense that if AC were held constant for a dative pair (like ((153) a) and ((153) b)), the GF assignment for one member of the pair would have to be illegal. For example, if the goal was always a general unrestricted argument (as it is in ((149) a)), then it could not legally be an OBL_{goal} as it is in ((153) a). On the other hand, if the goal were always semantically restricted, it could not legally be an OBJ as it is in ((153) b). In order for the observed GFs of a Dative pair to be legal, there must be a change in AC.

The body of the benefactive rule (formulated in (159)) is similar to the dative rule.

(159)   Benefactive Rule: benefactive is general unrestricted and theme or patient is OBJ2.[35]

4.2.3. Comparison to Other Treatments of Double Object Constructions

Since the Dative/Benefactive rules have received so much attention, it will be useful to compare the LFG account with AC to some other accounts of these rules. The treatments of the Dative/Benefactive rules in RG and Marantz (1984) are interesting because the theories are similar in may ways to LFG with AC, and some of the differences between the theories are highlighted by the treatment of the Dative/Benefactive rules.

In RG, the Dative/Benefactive rules involve advancement to 2. In the initial stratum, a double object dative sentence has a 2 (which is a theme) and a 3 (which is a goal). If 3-to-2 advancement applies, the 3 advances to 2 and the initial 2 becomes a 2-chômeur ((160) a). The benefactive rule is similar except that the initial stratum has a 2 and a benefactive ((160) b).

(160)a.   **RG Dative Rule**

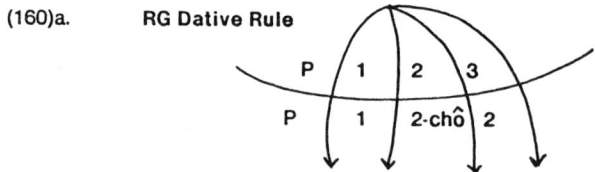

---

[35] The rule as formulated here will result in benefactives that are general unrestricted and will consequently take the OBJ function. At this time, I do not have an explanation for the failure of many benefactives to passivize.

b.   RG Benefactive Rule

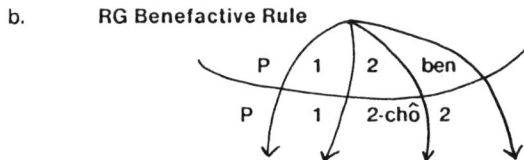

RG differs from LFG with AC in its inventory of grammatical functions. LFG does not have anything which corresponds to Relational Grammar's 3 relation. Initial 3s in RG are simply treated as semantically restricted arguments in LFG, and final 3s in RG are OBL_{goals} in LFG. It seems that part of the reason for having 3s in RG is that they often behave differently (i.e. undergo different rules) from other obliques. In LFG, any distinctive behavior of 3s in contrast to other obliques would be handled by a thematic rule which picks out a semantic class of verbs to apply to. So RG picks out these verbs by giving them a distinctive initial stratum while LFG gives them a relational representation that looks exactly like many other verbs and lets thematic relation changing rules sort them out semantically. For example, the Dative Rule in LFG is sensitive to the distinction between change of possession and directed motion. It applies to ((161) a) but not to ((162) a) in spite of the fact that the verbs in these sentences are identical at the level of argument clasification. In fact, they are identical at the level of predicate argument structure too — they each have an agent, a theme, and a goal. Recall that according to Jackendoff (1976), thematic roles are determined by the semantic class of a verb and many semantic classes can determine the same set of thematic roles. The Dative Rule is sensitive to the semantic class of change of possession verbs, not to the thematic roles agent, theme, and goal.

(161)a.   I sent a letter to my mother.
     b.   I sent my mother a letter.

(162)a.   I sent a letter to New York.
     b.   * I sent New York a letter.

It would be possible to incorporate the RG approach into LFG by introducing something analogous to 3 as an argument class. Then, as in RG, the Dative rule would apply to all verbs with 3s instead of picking out a semantic class to apply to. (Of course, the semantic class would be picked out by the rule that assigned the 3s.) However, this would be an unneccessary complication. The need for rules which refer to semantic classes of verbs is independently motivated by rules like the causative/inchoative rule. Given that the mechanism for semantically sensitive rules exists, and given that it *can* account for the distribution of dative pairs, there is no need for a new argument class to single out the dative rule verbs syntactically.

The success of LFG with respect to doing without 3s remains to be seen. Many constructions have been analyzed in RG with the use of 3s and I have not yet tried to reformulate all of them in terms of argument classifications.

Another RG relation which does not exist in LFG is chômeur. RG's 2-chômeurs are OBJ2s in LFG and RG's 1-chômeurs are OBL_{agent} in LFG. Again, many rules in RG used the chômeur relations and I have not yet attempted to reformulate all of them in LFG. However, a few comments are in order.

While a 2-chômeur is supposedly unemployed, an OBJ2 has the job of being a freely encoded GF. Bresnan (1982c) shows that OBJ2 does a lot of work as a lexically induced functional controller and as an anaphoric controllee. So Relational Grammarians will have to account for why a supposedly unemployed nominal is still active in these ways. (For example, it may work as an *acting 2* (Perlmutter 1982)).

On the other hand, Relational Grammarians point out numerous examples of properties which distinguish 2s from 2-chômeurs. These are usually things that 2s do and 2-chômeurs do not do. In LFG, the same facts would have to be formulated as differences between OBJ and OBJ2 and would preferably be motivated rather than just being stipulated. A weakness of LFG is that OBJ and OBJ2 are too similar — they are both freely encoded (or semantically unrestricted) functions that can attach to general unrestricted arguments. So the differences between them (e.g. the restricted distribution of OBJ2 and the absence of an OBJ2-to-SUBJ relation change in passivization) can be captured by explicitly referring to the difference between OBJ and OBJ2, but they are not really explained in the deeper sense of following from some difference in the definition of OBJ and OBJ2.

Notice that the difference between 1s and 1-chômeurs in RG corresponds to the difference between SUBJ and OBL_{agent} in LFG and the difference in behavior between these two functions *does* follow in a principled way from the definition of semantically encoded (or semantically restricted) functions and freely encoded (or semantically unrestricted) functions.

The RG use of chomage would take on some force if it turned out that 2-chômeurs and 1-chomeurs shared some behavior as a class which was not shared by other relations (aside from the fact that they do not do things that SUBJs and OBJs do). Again, this could be formulated, but not explained, in LFG because OBJ2 and OBL_{agent} do not form any sort of natural class and there is no principled reason for them to share any behavior.

In addition to the differences in the inventory of grammatical relations, the LFG Dative Rule differs from the RG Dative Rule in another way. In RG, the two members of a dative pair have the same initial stratum. So rules that apply to a double object sentence (e.g *Give me a book.*) have access to the fact that the final 2-chômeur was an intial 2 and the final 2 is an initial 3. In LFG, the lexical form for *give* in *give me a book* shows no indication that the goal (*me*) ever had a semantically restricted AC. In RG, many things have been explained in terms of the initial 3-hood of the goal argument in a double object sentence. These things will have to be explained in terms of thematic roles or in some other way in LFG.

Differences between Marantz's dative rule and the LFG dative rule lie in the status of the entities that the rule manipulates. The closest analog to the general unrestricted argument class in Marantz's theory is an element which gets a semantic role from a verb. However, Marantz considers it highly marked for a verb to assign two semantic roles (LFG, in contrast, does not treat the presence of two general unrestricted arguments as highly marked), and his dative rule does not result in two arguments getting semantic roles from the verb. Rather, the goal gets a role from the verb and the theme gets a role from its position as [NP, VP]. Since role assigners in Marantz's theory correspond to semantically encoded functions in LFG and since the position [NP, VP] corresponds to the function OBJ2, this is analogous to the claim that OBJ2 is a semantically encoded function. This claim is not accepted in LFG.

4.3. Patient Rule

The Patient Rule (Hale & Laughren 1983) produces lexical forms for the (b) sentences below. The (b) sentences, like the (a) sentences, contain an agent and a patient argument but, in contrast to the (a) sentences, the patient in the (b) sentences is oblique.

(163)a.　　I poked the potato.
　　　b.　　I poked at the potato.
(164)a.　　The hunter shot the bird.
　　　b.　　The hunter shot at the bird.

The Patient Rule must involve an alternate classification for patients because if the (a) and (b) sentences had the same ACs, then some well-formedness condition would have to be violated. If the patient were a general unrestricted argument in all sentences, then it could not legally be assigned to the function $OBL_{patient}$ (assuming that this is the function of the prepositional phrases in the (b) sentences) and if the AC of the patient were semantically restricted in all sentences, the assignment of OBJ in the (a) sentences would be illegal.

((165) a) formulates the Patient Rule and ((165) b) formulates another classification rule for patient arguments. The semantic domain for both rules, though not listed explicitly, is the class of verbs with patient arguments. Notice that the rules do not have to specify the GFs of the agent and patient because these are totally predictable from the normal operation of purely syntactic rules. Furthermore, the two classification rules do not have to specify a change in transitivity. ((165) b) will result in forms that have both a subjective unrestricted and a general unrestricted argument while ((165) a) will result in forms without a general unrestricted argument. According to Lexical Default 1, which determines that verbs with both an subjective unrestricted argument and a general unrestricted argument are usually transitive, the former will be transitive but the latter do not fall in the domain of application of this default rule and do not have to be transitive. ((166) a) and ((166) b) show the lexical forms for ((164) a) and ((164) b).

(165)a.   **Patient Rule:** Patient is semantically restricted.
    b.   Patient is general unrestricted.

(166)a.   'shoot< <u>agent</u> **patient** >'
                  SUBJ OBJ
               "The hunter shot the bird"

    b.   'shoot< <u>agent</u> **patient** >'
                  SUBJ OBL_{pat}
               "The hunter shot at the bird."

4.4. The Passive Rule

4.4.1. Formulation of the Rule

The passive rule in the theory of AC is a thematic rule which provides an alternate argument classification for certain arguments. In the unmarked case, it applies to the same arguments that would be subjective unrestricted in active sentences, though there are presumably some exceptions including verbs like *involve* and *include* which I discussed in Chapter 2. The passive rule formulated in (167) applies to agents but a more complete specification of the rule would include a longer list of roles. (167) coexists with (168), the classification rule for agents of active sentences. The semantic domain for both rules is the set of verbs with agent arguments.

(167)   **English Passive Rule:** Agent is semantically restricted.

(168)   Agent is subjective unrestricted.

((169) a and ((169) b) show the argument classifications for active and passive *kick*.

(169)a.   'kick< <u>agent</u> patient >'   *active*

b.   'kick< agent patient >'   *passive*

Passivization in the theory of AC applies at a different level of representation than it does in other versions of LFG. Instead of changing the grammatical function assignment directly, the Passive Rule produces an alternate argument classification. But since active and passive ACs get different GF assignments, the overall effect is that corresponding arguments in active and passive forms have different GFs.

4.4.2. The Passive Rule and Transitivity

Notice that the Passive Rule does not explicitly affect the transitivity of the verbs it applies to. Active forms like ((169) a) fall in the domain of Lexical Default Rule 1 and will, therefore, be transitive. Passive forms like ((169) b), on the other hand, have no subjective unrestricted argument and, according to Lexical Default Rule 2, can be either transitive or intransitive.

The requirement that lexical forms have SUBJs is the main factor in determining whether a passive verb will be intransitive. Since sentences must have SUBJs and since there is no longer a subjective unrestricted argument after passivization, the SUBJ must come from somewhere else, so it must be a general unrestricted argument or non-thematic (since these are the only other possibilities). If a passive form does not have a non-thematic subject, then SUBJ will have to be assigned to a general unrestricted argument and the resulting form will be intransitive. But if it does have a dummy subject, then the passive verb can be transitive and the general unrestricted argument can be an object.

The unmarked passive sentence in English is intransitive and contains a general unrestricted subject rather than a dummy subject, but this is not a property of the passive construction specifically. Since dummy subjects in English are all introduced by semantically conditioned thematic rules, they are more rare than non-dummy subjects.

In order to see the possible outcomes of the Passive Rule with and without dummy subjects, consider its effect on transitive verbs with general unrestricted objects and with non-thematic objects.

((169) b) is a lexical form for passive *kick* at the end of the thematic rule component, assuming that no dummy subject has been introduced. Lexical Default Rule 2 allows this form to be either transitive or intransitive but various other factors conspire to make it intransitive. If it were transitive, then SUBJ and OBJ would be competing for the general unrestricted argument because neither of them could legally be assigned anywhere else. Since function-argument biuniqueness prevents them from both attaching to the general unrestricted argument at the same time, one of them would go unassigned. If SUBJ is not assigned as in the derivation shown in ((170) b), then the Subject Condition will be violated and if OBJ is not assigned, the lexical form ((170) c) will also be ill-formed because it will have an unused subcategorized argument. On the other hand, if the lexical form were intransitive, SUBJ would get assigned to the general unrestricted argument and the resulting lexical form would be well-formed ((170) a).

(170) a.   'kick< agent patient >'   *p.a.s.*

        'kick< agent patient >'   *classification rules*

        'kick< agent patient >'   *transitivity*

        'kick< agent patient >'   *GF assignment*
              OBL_{ag} SUBJ

b.   'kick< agent patient >'   *p.a.s.*

        'kick< agent patient >'   *classification rules*

        'kick< agent patient >' OBJ   *transitivity*[36]

        'kick< agent patient >'   *GF assignment*
              OBL_{ag} OBJ

c.   'kick< agent patient >'   *p.a.s.*

        'kick< agent patient >'   *classification rules*

        'kick< agent patient >' OBJ   *transitivity*

        'kick< agent patient >' OBJ   *GF assignment*
              OBL_{ag} SUBJ

---

[36] I am assuming that the lexical default rules for transitivity create these partially specified lexical forms even though there is no well-formed way to complete them. What I have in mind is a system which generates all of the subcategorization frames for a lexical item. It starts with a predicate argument structure and applies all rules that are applicable. This will result in multiple derived partially specified lexical forms and all applicable rules will apply to each of them too. If one of the partially specified lexical forms cannot be completed in a well-formed way, then the derivation of that form simply goes no further and no reflex of that form will appear in the final set of subcategorization frames.

Passive raising-to-object verbs must also be intransitive when no expletive subject is assigned. If they were transitive, then the lexical rule of functional control would assign OBJ as the controller of XCOMP and SUBJ would remain unassigned ((171) a). If, on the other hand, passive raising-to-object verbs were intransitive, then OBJ would no longer be in the verb's subcategorization list and the lexical rule of functional control could assign SUBJ as the controller ((171) b).

(171)a. 'consider< considerer considered >'   p.a.s

  'consider< considerer *considered* >'   classification rules

  'consider< considerer *considered* >' OBJ   transitivity

  'consider< considerer *considered* >' OBJ   GF assignment
         OBL$_{ag}$ XCOMP

  'consider< considerer *considered* >'   Lexical Rule of
         OBL$_{ag}$ XCOMP   Functional Control

  (↑ OBJ) = (↑ XCOMP SUBJ)

b. 'consider< considerer considered >'   p.a.s

  'consider< considerer *considered* >'   classification rules

  'consider< considerer *considered* >'   transitivity

  'consider< considerer *considered* >'   GF assignment
         OBL$_{ag}$ XCOMP

  'consider< considerer *considered* >'   Lexical Rule of
         OBL$_{ag}$ XCOMP   Functional Control

  (↑ SUBJ) = (↑ XCOMP SUBJ)

In Chapter 3, I pointed out that raising-to-object verbs are idiosyncratically specified as transitive, but this statement requires modification in light of the passive construction. I assume that raising-to-object verbs carry an idiosyncratic specification that they are transitive when they have a subjective unrestricted argument. ((172) a) shows the predicate argument structure before argument classification, grammatical function assignment, or the lexical default rules for transitivity apply.

(172)a. 'consider< considerer considered >'

  Idiosyncratic specification of transitivity: transitive when there is a subjective unrestricted argument.

So far, I have shown that principles of the theory require passive verbs to be intransitive when no dummy subject is introduced. Now consider an example of the passive construction with a dummy subject. (173) shows the derivation for *enacted* in *There was enacted a battle between two fierce leaders*.[37] In the thematic rule component, two classification rules apply: one that puts the theme in the general unrestricted class and one (the Passive Rule) which puts the agent in the semantically restricted class. Next, the Pleonastic *There* Rule (next section) introduces *there* as a dummy subject. At this point, Lexical Default Rule 2 determines that the lexical form could be either transitive or intransitive but only the transitive option is shown here. The intransitive form could not be completed in a well-formed way because the general unrestricted argument could not get a function. (Assuming that something prevents OBJ2 from being assigned.) Finally, the purely syntactic rules assign OBJ to the theme, thereby creating a transitive passive verb.

A similar and more convincing analysis is proposed by Burzio (1981), and Baker (1983) for Italian sentences like *Furono arrestati molti studenti* (literally: were arrested many students). This sentence supposedly has a phonetically null dummy subject and an object *molti studenti* (many students).

(173) 'enact< agent theme >' *predicate argument structure*

'enact< agent theme >' *classification rules*

'enact< agent theme >' *Expletive There Rule*
($\uparrow$ SUBJ) = [U −, LOC +]
($\uparrow$ OBJ NUM) = ($\uparrow$ SUBJ NUM)
($\uparrow$ OBJ PERSON) = ($\uparrow$ SUBJ PERSON)

'enact< agent theme >' OBJ *Transitivity*
($\uparrow$ SUBJ) = [U −, LOC +]
($\uparrow$ OBJ NUM) = ($\uparrow$ SUBJ NUM)
($\uparrow$ OBJ PERSON) = ($\uparrow$ SUBJ PERSON)

'enact< agent theme >' *GF assignment*
       OBJ
($\uparrow$ SUBJ) = [U −, LOC +]
($\uparrow$ OBJ NUM) = ($\uparrow$ SUBJ NUM)
($\uparrow$ OBJ PERSON) = ($\uparrow$ SUBJ PERSON)

The same reasoning about transitivity holds for raising-to-object verbs, which have non-thematic objects in place of general unrestricted objects. If SUBJ gets assigned to a

---

[37] In the next section, I explain the difference between *There was enacted a battle* where *battle* is the OBJ of *enacted* and *There was a battle enacted* where *battle* is the OBJ of a special form of *be*. Another possibility is that the two sentences are related by the non-relation changing rule of Heavy NP Shift.

dummy element, then OBJ can remain as controller of an XCOMP. This does not happen in English because assignment of dummies is not productive and there happens not to be a rule that inserts dummies in this context. However, the theory predicts that in a language with productive dummy insertion there could be passives of raising-to-object verbs which have dummy subjects and raised objects. These sentences would be equivalent to *There is believed someone to have left*, except they would be grammatical.

I have shown that the Passive Rule is not directly responsible for the intransitivity of most passive verbs and that passive verbs can, in fact, be transitive in the right circumstances. The next subsection elaborates on this and other advantages of the Passive Rule as it is formulated here.

4.4.3. Advantages of a Subject Demotion Approach

Passivization in LFG with AC can be classified as a *subject demotion* account because the essence of it is the reclassification of the SUBJ. This approach has several advantages over an *object promotion* account in which the essence of passivization is the promotion of an object to subjecthood. In order to show this, I will compare passivization in LFG with AC to two other formulations of passivization from Bresnan (1982b, henceforth PLT) and Perlmutter & Postal (1983a, henceforth UCP) which are not primarily subject demotion rules.

Passivization in PLT is neither primarily a subject demotion nor an object promotion account. Instead, subject demotion and object promotion seem to have equal status. A modified version of the PLT passive rule is repeated here.

(174) $\quad$ SUBJ $\rightarrow$ OBL$_{ag}$/Ø
$\qquad$ OBJ $\rightarrow$ SUBJ

RG passivization as described in UCP is an object promotion account. A 2 advances to 1 causing the original 1 to go *en chômage*.

(175)

In both the PLT and the UCP accounts of passivization, object promotion is part of the passivization rule. However, object promotion appears in other contexts as well. It appears alone in RG as unaccusative advancement. And in LFG, it accompanies other rules such as middle formation and the causative/inchoative rule.

If OBJ promotion is not a separate rule in its own right, then it has to be explicitly invoked for each construction where it applies. This would not be so bad if it were not for the fact that these constructions all have something in common. Listing object promotion explicitly as a part of each construction fails to capture a generalization about the syntactic circumstances when object promotion can apply.

Along these lines, Baker (1983) argues that LFG should adopt a subject demotion account. He shows how a more elegant rule system in Italian results from factoring out the object-to-subject relation change from a number of rules. He proposes that object-to-subject applies after these rules instead of being a part of each one. Passivization in LFG with AC is based on this observation.

In LFG with AC, there is no rule which changes an explicit OBJ assignment into a SUBJ assignment, but there are circumstances under which a SUBJ takes on an assignment which would be taken by OBJ in related lexical forms where circumstances are different. This happens when there is no subjective unrestricted argument and no expletive has been assigned as a value for SUBJ. These circumstances can be created by many rules — including passivization, middle formation, and the causative/inchoative rule — and they can arise in the basic form of unaccusative verbs. The assignment of SUBJ to a general unrestricted argument (or to a non-thematic element which is normally an OBJ) is not part of any of these rules. The advantages of separating it out as a separate process are (1) reduction in redundancy in the formulation of various rules and (2) capturing a generalization about the circumstances when SUBJ can take an assignment usually reserved for OBJ.

There are two additional reasons for believing that OBJ promotion is not part of passivization: sometimes it does not occur when passivization does and sometimes passivization applies when there is no OBJ to advance.

Examples where OBJ promotion does not accompany passivization were cited above in (173). These are not surprising in LFG with AC because OBJ promotion is not part of passivization. They would also not be surprising for the PLT account of passivization if the OBJ promotion part of the rule were made optional. However, the treatment of these sentences in RG is slightly more complex: in order for passivization to include an advancement, a dummy element must be introduced which bumps the original 2 into chômage and then advances to 1 (Rosen 1981).

Passivization of intransitive verbs (in languages that allow it) results in an impersonal passive construction. In LFG with AC, impersonal passivization is simply the expected result of applying passivization to an intransitive verb.[38] It is not surprising that passivization applies in the absence of OBJs because object promotion and detransitivization are not part of the rule. In Chapter 5, I discuss the impersonal passive construction in Dutch.

Again, PLT-style passivization could cover the impersonal passive if object promotion were made optional. And again, the RG account is slightly more complex. In order to have object promotion, a dummy 2 is introduced which advances to 1.

Subject demotion accounts of passivization have four attractive features: they reduce redundancy in rule systems; they capture generalizations about when object promotion applies; they extend easily to cases of passivization where an object does not promote; and they extend easily to cases of passivization where there is no object. There are, however, some potential advantages of an object promotion account.

The 1-Advancement Exclusiveness Law (Perlmutter & Postal 1984) accounts for the unpassivizability of many predicates by limiting the number of promotions (advancements) in a derivation. I will return to this in Chapter 5 where I present a subject-demotion account of unpassivizable predicates in Dutch.

Languages which do not have an impersonal passive present another potential problem for subject demotion accounts of the passive construction. Under a subject demotion account, nothing special has to be done in order to allow passive to apply to intransitive verbs, but there is no natural way to prevent the passive rule from applying to intransitive verbs in languages that do not have impersonal passives. As I have set things up here, I cannot simply constrain the passive rule to apply to transitive verbs because the passive rule is a classification rule and transitivity is not yet determined at the point when classification rules apply. (The Lexical Default Rules determine transitivity on the basis of argument classification and therefore must come after argument classification.) The modified passive rule for English in (176) will not apply to intransitive verbs. It reclassifies an agent when there is a general unrestricted argument and when there is an idiosyncratic condition on transitivity like the one in ((172) a). The overall effect is that (176) will apply to forms which would be transitive in other circumstances.

---

[38] In some languages the personal and impersonal passive are not so closely related and would be better treated as separate rules. Turkish may be such a language (Knecht in preparation).

(176) English Passive Rule: Agent is semantically restricted or unexpressed.

[*Applies to verbs with general unrestricted arguments and to verbs with idiosyncratic transitivity conditions.*]

4.5. Inversion Constructions in English

In English, there is a rather marked construction involving a fronted prepositional phrase (or the locative pronominals *here* and *there*) and a post verbal NP, which in the unmarked word order, would have been in the usual preverbal subject position. I will refer to this construction as *oblique inversion*.[39]

(177)a. Between the trees twinkled lights of cottage candles and far down flared bright windows of the village stores. (RPSp15)
   b. Lights of cottage candles twinkled between the trees and bright windows of the village stores flared far down.
(178)a. And from the little windows of the barn projected bobbing heads of bays and blacks and sorrels. (RPSp19).
   b. Bobbing heads of bays and blacks and sorrels projected from the little windows of the barn.

Many English speakers would balk at the thought of calling the preposed PPs subjects in the (a) sentences above. And in one respect they would be right. The preposed PPs do not behave like subjects with respect to c-structure phenomena such as subject-auxiliary inversion. But with respect to at least one f-structure process, raising-to-subject, they do behave like subjects. In fact, in this respect, their distribution is similar to that of the pleonastic element *there*.

I claim in this chapter that the fronted PPs above are SUBJs but that they sometimes fail tests for subjecthood because they are oblique. In Chapter 5, I will point out similarities between fronted PPs in English and fronted non-nominative NPs (often referred to as *quirky case-marked subjects*) in Dutch and other languages.

In this chapter, I will discuss the similarity between oblique inversion and the use of pleonastic *there* in English. I will concentrate on the less commonly used sentences where *there* precedes a verb other than *be*.

---

[39] Many examples in this section are taken from texts abbreviated as follows:

RPS = Zane Grey, *Riders of the Purple Sage*, in *Zane Grey: Five Complete Novels*,

LWS = Zane Grey, *The Light of the Western Stars*

SM = Somerset Maugham, *The Moon and Sixpence*

(179)a. Up in the attic of this little house there lived a ghost.[40]
b. There came a moment when a blacker shade overspread the wide area of flickering gleams and obliterated them. (LWSp138)

Subsection 4.5.1 contains a formulation of the oblique inversion and pleonastic *there* constructions in terms of AC and Subsection 4.5.2 deals with the problem of mixed subjecthood behavior of fronted PPs and pleonastic *there*. I show that the theory of control in LFG correctly predicts that oblique and pleonastic subjects should pass some tests for subjecthood and fail others.

4.5.1. Formulation of English Inversion Rules

In Chapter 2, I showed that the pleonastic *there* construction follows the usual pattern of URs: pleonastic *there* is used with passive verbs and some intransitive verbs but it is not used with transitive verbs or with other intransitive verbs. The same observation holds for oblique inversion. Sentences ((177) a) and ((178) a) show the intransitive verbs *twinkle* and *project* in the oblique inversion construction and sentences ((180) a) and ((180) b) show passive verbs in the oblique inversion construction. In ((180) b) oblique inversion has applied in the relative clause.

(180)a. Here in the stone wall, had been wonderfully carved by wind or washed by water several deep caves above the level of the terrace. (RPS p.58)
b. Imagine a board on which is written a long equation with many variables.

The ungrammatical sentences in ((181) a) and ((181) b) are attempts to apply oblique inversion to an unergative verb and a transitive verb.

(181)a. * At the party danced many girls with their boyfriends.
b. * At the party kissed many girls their boyfriends.

The patterning of the pleonastic *there* and oblique inversion constructions as URs follows from the AC of the post verbal NP. This NP is a general unrestricted argument and therefore can be a SUBJ, as in ((177) b) and ((178) b), or it can be an OBJ. Thus, it appears to undergo a SUBJ/OBJ relation change. Inversion constructions (including oblique inversion and the pleonastic *there* construction) arise when these arguments take the OBJ function. Transitive verbs with subjective unrestricted SUBJs do not participate in inversion constructions because their SUBJs, being subjective unrestricted, cannot undergo a

---

[40] Robert Bright, *Georgie*, Scholastic Book Services, New York, 1944.

SUBJ/OBJ relation change. For the same reason, unergative verbs do not undergo any kind of inversion. Passive verbs, on the other hand, do participate in inversion constructions because they have no subjective unrestricted argument and therefore their general unrestricted argument can undergo a SUBJ/OBJ relation change. And, of course, unaccusative verbs undergo inversion in the same way.[41]

When the general unrestricted argument of an inversion verb takes the OBJ function, some other value must be introduced to take the SUBJ function. One possible value for SUBJ in this situation is pleonastic *there* which is encoded by the constraint equation $(\uparrow SUBJ) =_c [LOC +, U -]$. This constraint will only be satisfied if the word *there* appears in SUBJ position in c-structure. The lexical entry for pleonastic *there* is shown in ((182) a). The absence of a PRED feature indicates that it is pleonastic and the minus value for the U feature indicates that *there* has phonetic content. That is, it is not unexpressed.

(182)a.   *there*: $(\uparrow LOC) = +$
            $(\uparrow U) = -$

I suggest here that oblique phrases can also serve as pleonastic subjects in the sense that they have no value for SUBJ PRED (Andrews 1982). This assumes a layered representation of PPs in f-structure consisting of a case marker and an OBJ whose value is a sub-f-structure. (184) shows the f-structure for the sentence *The children walked to school*. Rule (183) is responsible for building the OBL_{goal} f-structure corresponding to the phrase *to*

---

[41] If the post-verbal NP in inverted sentences is an OBJ, then we have to explain why it has a strong tendency to occur at the end of the sentence to the right of whatever PPs may be present. I suggest the NPs in question are OBJs and that discourse factors conspire to force the application of Heavy NP Shift.

school.[42]

(183)

$$PP \rightarrow \begin{array}{cc} P & NP \\ \uparrow = \downarrow & (\uparrow OBJ) = \downarrow \end{array}$$

(184)

$$\begin{bmatrix} SUBJ & \begin{bmatrix} PRED & \text{'child'} \\ NUM & pl \\ PERS & 3 \\ SPEC & def \end{bmatrix} \\ PRED & \text{'walk} \langle SUBJ \; OBL_{goal} \rangle\text{'} \\ TENSE & past \\ OBL_{goal} & \begin{bmatrix} CASE & OBL_{goal} \\ OBJ & \begin{bmatrix} PRED & \text{'school'} \\ NUM & sg \\ PERS & 3 \end{bmatrix} \end{bmatrix} \end{bmatrix}$$

Phrase structure rule (185) describes the structure of oblique inversion sentences. And

---

[42]Bresnan (1982c) proposes a flat representation for OBL phrases which are headed in f-structure by the PRED from the NP that they contain. Using this representation for obliques, the f-structure for *The children walked to school* would be as follows.

$$\begin{bmatrix} SUBJ & \begin{bmatrix} PRED & \text{'child'} \\ NUM & PL \\ PERS & 3 \\ SPEC & def \end{bmatrix} \\ PRED & \text{'walk} \langle SUBJ \; OBL_{go} \rangle\text{'} \\ TENSE & past \\ OBL_{go} & \begin{bmatrix} PRED & \text{'school'} \\ CASE & OBL_{go} \\ NUM & sg \\ PERS & 3 \end{bmatrix} \end{bmatrix}$$

The choice of representations for obliques should be partly determined by data concerning possible antecedents of anaphorically controlled clauses. This data at first seems to confirm the flat representation of oblique phrases. For example, in the sentence *Contradicting himself appealed to Mr. Jones*, *Mr. Jones* is a possible anaphoric controller for the phrase *contradicting himself*. According to the theory of control proposed in Bresnan (1982c), antecedents of anaphoric control must f-command the controlled clause. If *to Mr. Jones* had a flat representation in f-structure, it would f-command the controlled clause, but if the PP had a layered structure, *Mr. Jones* would be too far embedded to f-command the controlled clause.

Even though it seems that the flat representation of obliques makes the correct prediction about anaphoric control by prepositional objects, it is possible to change the definition of f-command slightly in order to get the right results using the non-flat representation of PPs. I suggest the following definition of f-command: X f-commands Y if X does not contain Y and every *clause nucleus* (the old definition said *f-structure* here) that contains X contains Y. Under this definition, *Mr. Jones* will f-command *contradicting himself* even assuming the layered representation of PPs.

(186) shows the lexical form of a verb that participates in oblique inversion. Notice that it looks rather similar to a verb which occurs in the pleonastic *there* construction. This verb will not be able to occur with meaningful NP subjects for two reasons. First, the SUBJ function is non-thematic and any NP that filled that function would not receive a thematic role. And second, such an NP, if all of its features were spelled out, would presumably conflict with the plus value for the LOC feature. The features specified for SUBJ in (186) will successfully merge with features supplied by the PP in (185).

(185)
$$S \rightarrow \begin{array}{cccc} (PP) & (NP) & & VP \\ (\uparrow SUBJ) = \downarrow & (\uparrow SUBJ) = \downarrow & & \uparrow = \downarrow \\ \left\{ \begin{array}{c} (\uparrow (\downarrow CASE)) = \downarrow \\ \downarrow \epsilon (\uparrow ADJUNCTS) \end{array} \right\} & & & \end{array}$$

(186) $(\uparrow PRED) = $ 'dwell< theme loc >'
                                    OBJ   OBL$_{loc}$

$(\uparrow SUBJ) = \begin{bmatrix} U & - \\ LOC & + \end{bmatrix}$

$(\uparrow SUBJ\ CASE)$

Notice that although the fronted PP in (185) has two functions (SUBJ and OBL or SUBJ and ADJUNCT), this is not a violation of function-argument biuniqueness. Function-argument biuniqueness states that each thematic role has no more than one grammatical function and each grammatical function has no more than one thematic role. This condition is satisfied by (186). In other words, the construction is permissable because nothing prevents a phrase from having two functions provided that one of them is non-thematic.

The rules and lexical entries above result in the following f-structure for the oblique inversion sentence *Among them dwelt a man of consequence.*

(187)
$$\begin{bmatrix} SUBJ & \begin{bmatrix} CASE & OBL_{loc} \\ OBJ & \begin{bmatrix} PRED & \text{'pro'} \\ NUM & pl \\ PERS & 3 \end{bmatrix} \end{bmatrix} \\ OBL_{loc} & \\ PRED & \text{'dwell< OBJ\ OBL}_{loc}\text{ >'} \\ TENSE & past \\ OBJ & \begin{bmatrix} \text{"a man of consequence"} \end{bmatrix} \end{bmatrix}$$

A final detail of the formulation of inversion constructions involves agreement with the post verbal NP. Following suggestions made at an LFG workshop on Icelandic case marking (Center for the Study of Language and Information, Stanford University, June 1984), I assume that equations may be introduced that allow a verb to agree with an OBJ when the SUBJ is not suitable for agreement in some way. In the case of the oblique inversion and pleonastic *there* constructions, the SUBJ is unsuitable for agreement because it lacks number and person features. A more complete lexical entry for *dwells* is given in (188).

(188) 'dwell< theme **loc** >'
         OBJ   OBL$_{goal}$
    ($\uparrow$ SUBJ) = [LOC +, U −]
    ($\uparrow$ SUBJ CASE)
    ($\uparrow$ OBJ NUM) = sg
    ($\uparrow$ OBJ PERSON) = 3
    ($\uparrow$ TENSE) = PRES

4.5.2. Subjecthood of Fronted PPs and Pleonastic *There*

In this subsection, I discuss the subjecthood of fronted PPs and pleonastic *there*. The basic issue concerning these phrases is that they seem to be subjects in some respects and not in others. The possible resolutions of the issue are (1) that they are SUBJs in which case we need to explain why they fail certain tests for subjecthood (2) that they are not SUBJs, in which case we need to explain why they pass certain tests for subjecthood or (3) that there is something wrong with the notion of SUBJ. I take the first approach here and I show that they theory of control automatically explains why oblique and pleonastic subjects fail certain subjecthood tests.

I believe that it is important to draw a connection between pleonastic subjects and oblique subjects when it comes to questions of mixed subjecthood behavior. Pleonastic *there* is generally agreed to be a SUBJ, but the subjecthood of oblique phrases in various languages is more controversial. I show in this subsection that obliques and pleonastics are quite similar in their patterns of subjecthood behavior and I conclude that the subjecthood of oblique phrases should be no more controversial than the subjecthood of pleonastic elements.

In this section I will use control as a test for subjecthood. In control structures, a non-tensed verb is separated from its functional SUBJ. The understood SUBJ of *have eaten their vegetables* in ((189) a) is found in c-structure in the subject position of the matrix verb *seem*, the understood SUBJ of *being an important executive* in ((189) f) is structurally found in the S to which that phrase is adjoined, and so on. Since only SUBJs can be controlled in English, I will conclude that anything that is controlled is a SUBJ.

(189) a. The children seem to have eaten their vegetables.
b. We believe the children to have eaten their vegetables.
c. The children expect to have eaten their vegetables.
d. Attaining the respect of the president is the goal of every executive.
e. To attain the respect of the president is the goal of every executive.
f. Being an important executive, Jane had no reason to worry about her future.

Verbs taking the dummy subject *there* appear in one of these constructions, but are totally inconceivable in the others.

(190) a. There seemed to come a time when there was nothing more to do.
b. The children believe there to have come a time when candy grows on trees.
c. * There expect to live in our town people of great importance.
d. * Having been people in the room was comforting.
(With the reading *There having been people in the room was comforting*)
e. * To come a time of peace is important.
(With the reading *For there to come a time of peace is important*)
f. * Running from our humble well water fit for kings, there is no reason to worry.
(With the reading *There running from our humble well...*)[43]

If controllability is considered to be a property of subjects, and *there* cannot be controlled in many instances, we might conclude that *there* is not a full fledged subject. Instead, I claim that the possibility of controlling *there* in at least one control structure indicates that it is a subject but the properties that distinguish *there* as a dummy subject prevent it from being controlled in the other structures.

Fronted PPs in oblique inversion constructions are similar to pleonastic *there* in their ability to be controlled:

(191) a. Among them seemed to dwell many people of consequence.
b. * We believe among them to dwell a man of consequence.
c. * Among them expected to dwell many people of consequence.
d. * (Among them) having dwelt many people of consequence, they had no reason to worry about being overlooked.
e. * (Among them) to dwell many people of consequence would be nice.

Again, the fact that fronted PPs can be controlled in one construction indicates that

---

[43] This sentence is not very good, but it is not due to a general restriction against *there* in adjunct clauses, as evidenced by the grammaticality of *There being water in the well, there was no reason to worry* and *With there running from our humble well water fit for kings...*)

they are SUBJs but we are left with the problem of explaining why they cannot be controlled in other constructions. Fortunately, the apparently sporadic control behavior of pleonastic *there* and fronted PPs begins to make sense when we separate out the different types of control and examine how they are encoded in f-structure.

The sentences in ((189) a-(189) f) illustrate three types of control: anaphoric control, functional control by a thematic argument of the matrix clause, and functional control by a non-thematic element of the matrix clause.[44]

Sentences ((189) d) and ((189) e) contain the anaphorically controlled phrases *attaining the respect of the president* and *to attain the respect of the president*. These phrases, although they have no c-structure subject, are supplied with a functional subject which has the value PRO for the PRED feature. This PRO subject is introduced in the lexical entries for non-finite verbs. For example, the verb *attaining* in ((189) d) would have the lexical entry shown in (192). When this verb appears without a phrase structure subject, a functional subject is supplied by the (optional) equation (↑ SUBJ) = [PRED PRO, U +]. The plus value for U indicates that the subject of this verb is unexpressed.

(192)   'attain< <u>agent</u> theme >'
                  SUBJ OBJ
          (↑ PARTICIPLE) = PRES
          (↑ SUBJ) = [PRED PRO, U +]

Anaphoric control is inconsistent with the pleonastic *there* and oblique inversion constructions in two ways. First, the lexical entries for pleonastic *there* and oblique inversion verbs specify the value minus for the U feature but the features for anaphorically controlled PRO include the value plus for the U feature. Second, the anaphoric control equation shown in (192) introduces a PRED value for the anaphorically controlled subject but pleonastic *there* and oblique inversion verbs have non-thematic subjects. Introducing the equation (↑ SUBJ) = [PRED PRO, U +] into the lexical entry for an oblique inversion or pleonastic *there* verb could only result in semantically incoherent f-structures because the SUBJ of these verbs is not associated with a thematic argument slot and therefore the SUBJ's PRED would never be attached to a thematic argument slot. Thus, a consequence of the LFG treatment of anaphoric control is that pleonastic *there* and fronted PPs cannot be anaphorically controlled. Hence the ungrammaticality of ((190) d-((190) f) and ((191) d-((191) e).

---

[44] Mohanan (1983) considers ((189) f) to be an instance of a fourth type of control — constructionally induced functional control. Following Bresnan (1982c), I consider it to be another instance of anaphoric control because, like other anaphorically controlled clauses, the controlled clause does not need an antecedent in the same sentence: *Being an important executive, it seemed that the road to success had been easy.*

Sentences ((189) a-(189) c) are examples of functional control. Functionally controlled phrases also have nothing sitting in the usual c-structure position for subjects, but they get their functional subjects via a control equation. In these particular examples, the control equations are associated with the matrix verbs *seem*, *expect* (intransitive), and *believe*.

(193) a. 'seem< theme > SUBJ'
                          XCOMP
           (↑ SUBJ) = (↑ XCOMP SUBJ)

    b. 'believe< <u>agent</u> theme > OBJ'
                         SUBJ XCOMP
           (↑ OBJ) = (↑ XCOMP SUBJ)

    c. 'expect< <u>agent</u> theme >'
                        SUBJ XCOMP
           (↑ SUBJ) = (↑ XCOMP SUBJ)

In ((189) a) and ((189) c), the XCOMP of *seem* and *expect* is the phrase *to have eaten their vegetables*. This phrase has no overt subject but the control equation (↑ SUBJ) = (↑ XCOMP SUBJ) states that at the level of f-structure, the SUBJ of the XCOMP will be identical to the SUBJ of the matrix clause, thus a functional SUBJ is supplied to *to have eaten their vegetables*.

The difference between *seem* and *expect* is that the SUBJ of *expect* is a thematic argument of *expect*, but the SUBJ of *seem* is not a thematic argument of *seem*. For this reason, pleonastic *there* and oblique inversion sentences can be embedded under *seem* but not under *expect*. Fronted PPs and pleonastic *there* would not meet the semantic selectional restrictions of *expect*. Therefore, sentences ((190) c) and ((191) c) are ungrammatical.

Believe is similar to *seem* in that the controller of the XCOMP, OBJ in this case, is not a thematic argument in the main clause. Since *believe* does not impose semantic selectional restrictions on its OBJ, pleonastic *there* and fronted PPs should be able to occur under *believe*. It turns out, though, that while pleonastic *there* can be controlled under *believe* (as in ((190) b)), fronted PPs cannot be ((191) b). The reason for this is simply structural; the controller of the XCOMP of *believe* is generated in the main clause under an NP node labelled OBJ and the OBJ of *believe* cannot be a PP. Notice, though, that when *believe* is passivized its surface SUBJ is the controller of the XCOMP and oblique inversion is again possible.

(194)   Among them were believed to dwell many people of consequence.

The data in this subsection show that control constructions do not disprove the subjecthood of pleonastic *there* and fronted PPs. Rather, the formulations of these constructions actually predict that pleonastic *there* and fronted PPs should not be controllable in certain constructions even if they are subjects. In this way we can explain the mixed subjecthood behavior of pleonastic *there* and fronted PPs. They behave like subjects in some constructions because they are subjects and they fail to behave like subjects in other constructions because of their category or lack of PRED value.

Chapter 5
Formulation of Rules: Dutch

The purpose of this chapter is to formulate the three Dutch Unaccusative Rules (URs) which I discussed in Chapter 2. Section 5.1 deals with the passive construction in Dutch and includes an account of the unpassivizability of certain predicates. In Section 5.2, I argue that both the nominative and the dative NPs in experiencer inversion sentences are general unrestricted arguments and that they take turns being SUBJ and OBJ. Subsection 5.2.4 goes into some detail about the subjecthood of the dative NP. I argue, as I did for English oblique inversion, that non-nominative subjects may fail tests for subjecthood because of their case marking and that the theory should predict which tests they will pass and which ones they will fail. Section 5.3 formulates auxiliary selection as a UR, and points out a problem: the verbs which are unaccusative according to auxiliary selection are not the same as the verbs which are unaccusative according to the passive rule. The possible resolutions of this *mismatch* lead to a discussion of the status of AC as a level of representation.

5.1. Passivization

5.1.1. Formulation of the Dutch Passive Rule

We saw in Chapter 2 that the Passive Rule in Dutch is a UR: in addition to applying to transitive verbs, it also applies to some intransitive verbs ((195) a-(195) d), but not to all of them ((196) a-(196) c). Furthermore, it does not apply to already passive verbs. The following sentences are taken from Perlmutter (1978).

(195) a. Er wordt hier door de jonge lui veel gedanst. (P 32)
          "It is danced here a lot by the young people"
      b. Er wordt in deze kamer vaak geslapen. (P 35)
          "It is often slept in this room"
      c. Over dit problem wordt (er) vaak gesproken/gepraat/gedacht. (P 36)
          "About this problem it is often spoken/talked/thought."
      d. Er wordt geniesd/gehoest/gehikt. (P 42)
          "It is (being) sneezed/coughed/hiccoughed."

(196)a. *Door de lijken werd al gerot/ontbonden. (P 51a)
         "By the corpses it was already rotten/decomposed"
     b. *Uit dit weeshuis wordt (er) door vele kinderen verdwenen. (P 61a)
         "From this orphanage it is disappeared by many children"
     c. *Hier werd er door zulke dingen nooit gebeurd. (P 65b)
         "Here it was never happened by such things"

The Dutch Passive Rule is simpler than the English Passive Rule in that it does not have to be prevented from applying to intransitive verbs. As formulated in (197), it applies to verbs with agents whether they are transitive or intransitive. Note that a more complete formulation would include a longer list of passivizable thematic roles and this list would not necessarily be the same as the list of roles which undergo passive in English.

(197)   **Dutch Passive Rule:** Agent is semantically restricted or unexpressed.

Derivation of personal passives in Dutch is identical to derivation of passive verbs in English and so is not illustrated here. Example (198) illustrates the derivation of an impersonal passive in Dutch. The value $+/-$ for the U feature indicates that the dummy subject *er* is optionally expressed. A discussion of the circumstances under which it is expressed and not expressed is beyond the scope of this thesis.

(198)   'dansen< agent >'   P.A.S.

         'dansen< agent >'   passivization

         'dansen< agent >'   GF assignment
                  OBL_{ag}

         'dansen< agent >'   Dummy SUBJ assignment
                  OBL_{ag}
         $(\uparrow SUBJ) = \begin{bmatrix} U^{ag} +/- \\ LOC + \end{bmatrix}$

5.1.2. The 1-Advancement Exclusiveness Law

In Chapter 4, I compared two main approaches to the passive rule: the subject-demotion approach where the essence of passivization is the subject/oblique relation change and the object-promotion approach where the essence of passivization is the object/subject relation change. I pointed out that the English and Dutch passive rules presented here are subject-demotion rules because, although they do not explicitly change the function of a SUBJ, they do so indirectly by providing an alternate argument classification for arguments which would otherwise be SUBJs. I also argued that subject-demotion accounts of passivization are desirable because they provide a simple unified account of the personal and impersonal passive constructions.

In contrast, Perlmutter and Postal (1984) argue that the unpassivizability of certain predicates has a natural explanation in terms of an object-promotion passive rule along with the 1-Advancement Exclusiveness Law (1AEX). The 1AEX (formulated in RG terminology) rules out clauses where there has been more than one advancement to 1. For example, passivizing an unaccusative clause would involve first advancing the initial 2 to 1 (Unaccusative Advancement) and then advancing a dummy 2 to 1 (Impersonal Passivization). Since this derivation would include two advancements to 1, it is prohibited by the 1AEX. Similarly, already passive verbs cannot undergo passivization because the first application of passivization involves an advancement of 2 to 1 which precludes the second advancement of a dummy 2 to 1 (for an impersonal passive).

In spite of the fact that the 1AEX was formulated in object-promotion terms, it is possible to capture the unpassivizability of certain predicates in terms of a subject-demoting passive rule. In the theory of AC, the passive rule is inherently restricted because it is a classification rule; it classifies only certain designated arguments as semantically restricted or unexpressed. The Passive rule does not apply to unaccusative verbs because they do not have a thematic argument which is included in the list of passivizable arguments which is specified by the rule. For example, intransitive verbs with theme arguments do not passivize because theme is not one of the roles which the passive rule classifies. So, in the theory of AC, the thematic nature of the passive rule is what prevents it from applying to many verbs.

5.1.3. Syntactic and Semantic Properties of Unpassivizable Predicates

The passive rule presented here differs strikingly in one respect from the passive rule in other syntactic theories. In other theories, the input to passivization is specified in terms of syntactic entities like SUBJ and OBJ in LFG or 1 and 2 in RG. However, I have formulated passivization here as a clasification rule whose input is defined in terms of thematic roles like agent. Thus while the usual LFG passive rule applies to SUBJ, replacing it with OBL, the passive rule that I suggest here applies to agents (and other roles), classifying them as semantically restricted.

In this subsection, I address two issues: whether there are syntactic generalizations about the class of passivizable predicates which are not captured by my thematicaly defined passive rule and, more generally, what kind of evidence bears on the decision to define a rule thematically instead of syntactically. I begin by showing how a thematically defined passive rule can capture what appears to be a syntactic generalization about passivization.

In Chapter 2, I defined canonical subjects as those arguments which could be SUBJs but could not be OBJs in any related sentence. So, for example, the agent argument of *kick* is a canonical subject because it can be a SUBJ but no relation changing rule ever assigns the OBJ function to it. In some syntactic theories, canonical subjects are represented syntactically and they are syntactically prevented from becoming objects. For example, in AC, canonical subjects are represented as subjective unrestricted arguments which, by definition, cannot take the OBJ function and in GB, canonical subjects are deep structure subjects and the projection principle prevents them from moving into the verb phrase.

Now, it turns out that there is a connection between passivization and canonical subjects namely, that each passive verb corresponds to an active verb with a canonical subject. That is, there are passives corresponding to active transitive verbs and unergative verbs but there are no passives corresponding to unaccusative verbs or other passive verbs. Since canonical subjects are syntactically defined, it seems that this is a syntactic restriction on passivization and it looks like passivization should be defined syntactically. In fact, in an earlier draft of this thesis, I defined passivization as a lexical redundancy rule which applied to verbs that already had subjective unrestricted arguments and *re*classified them as semantically restricted. However, there is another way of looking at the issue.

In terms of argument classification, the relevant generalization about passivization is that arguments which can be classified as canonical subjects can also be classified as semantically restricted. I represent this in AC by having two classification rules which apply to the same set of arguments. Any argument which is classified as subjective unrestricted by one rule is alternately classified as semantically restricted by the other. And, any argument which cannot be classified as subjective unrestricted by the active classification rule cannot be classified as semantically restricted by the passive classification rule. Thus, instead of classifying subjective unrestricted arguments and then changing them into semantically restricted arguments, I simply classify them alternately as subjective unrestricted or semantically restricted. In this way, the passive rule in (197), whose domain of application is semantically defined, actually captures a syntactic generalization about the relationship between passives and canonical subjects.

We can extend this line of reasoning to account for why passives of Dutch transitive verbs do not repassivize as impersonal passives (another fact which is explained by the 1AEX in RG). In order for this to happen, an unlikely set of conditions would have to be satisfied. The first application of passivization would require an argument which could be subjective unrestricted or semantically restricted according to the active and passive classification rules. Then the second application of passivization would require another such argument. The existence of two passivizable arguments for a single lexical form is very unlikely and I assume that the situation does not arise.[45]

Now consider another potential objection to a semantically defined passive rule. Recall that I explained the unpassivizability of unaccusative verbs by appealing to their thematic structure. I said that they do not passivize because they do not have the thematic arguments which the passive rule requires. This amounts to saying that the passive rule distinguishes between unaccusative verbs and unergative verbs on semantic grounds rather than on syntactic grounds.

In contrast, Rosen (1981, 1982) argues that unaccusative verbs cannot be distinguished on purely semantic grounds from unergative verbs. She presents examples of nearly synonymous verbs from the same language one of which seems to be unergative while the other seems to be unaccusative. These examples presumably show that initial grammatical relations (and hence unergativity) cannot be totally predicted from semantic properties of predicates. In the system that Rosen suggests, URs would all have very clean syntactic formulations — they would all refer syntactically to the difference between predicates with initial 1's and predicates with initial 2's. Notice however, that the rules which assign initial grammatical relations will have to deal with the exceptional cases of nearly synonymous verbs with different syntactic behavior.

In the system that I propose here, some URs are formulated syntactically in terms of general unrestricted and subjective unrestricted arguments. Others, however, such as the passive rule, are formulated semantically. Rosen's minimal pairs, therefore, must be listed as exceptions to the passive rule. This seems at first to be a loss of generalization, but actually, recall that exceptions are typical of thematic rules in the theory of AC. Of course, one has to be careful not to abuse them by listing extraordinarily large numbers of them. But, in this case the minimal pairs which serve as exceptions are few and far between. Exceptions, therefore, do not strain the semantically defined passive rule in the theory of AC.

---

[45] Some verbs have multiple senses which have different passivizable arguments. For example, we can say *The apartment was rented by the tenant* or *The apartment was rented by the real estate office*. But each sense of *rent* has only one passivizable argument.

Furthermore, my treatment of exceptions is not as different from Rosen's as it seems at first. As I mentioned above, in an account like Rosen's, apparently synonymous minimal pairs must be handled by the rules that assign initial grammatical relations. These rules will have to assign the 1 relation to one argument while assigning the 2 relation to a semantically identical argument of another verb. Notice that classification rules in AC play an equivalent role to the rules that assign initial grammatical relations in RG, and, as in RG, exceptions to rules are handled at this point in the theory of AC. The difference between RG and LFG with AC is that many rules which explicitly change grammatical relations in RG are treated in LFG with AC as rules which create alternate argument classifications.

5.2. Experiencer Inversion

In this section, I will describe Experiencer Inversion as a construction in Dutch, but I will also discuss it in the larger context of inversion rules across languages. In particular, I will concentrate on one property of inversion constructions: the presence of a non-nominative NP which passes some tests for subjecthood and not others. This property has seemed puzzling and has led people in other syntactic theories to introduce new theoretical constructs (like the notion of Working 1 in RG (Perlmutter 1979)) or at least to question certain parts of the theory (like the idea that move-NP cannot apply to NPs with case in GB (Hoekstra 1984)). Nevertheless, I will show that LFG with AC leads to a simple and explanatory account of the syntactic properties of inversion constructions without the addition of extra aparatus or other perturbation to the theory.

5.2.1. Formalization of Dutch Experiencer Inversion

In Chapter 2, I showed that Dutch experiencer inversion is a UR by demonstrating that it only applies to verbs which do not have canonical subjects. The evidence supporting this took the form of three correct predictions. First, if experiencer inversion applies to verbs without canonical subjects and passivization applies to verbs with canonical subjects, then verbs which passivize should not undergo experiencer inversion. Second, for the same reason, verbs which undergo experiencer inversion should not passivize. And, finally, since passive verbs do not have canonical subjects, they should be able to undergo experiencer inversion as long as they have whatever other properties are required by the experiencer inversion construction. In Chapter 2, I presented data supporting each of these predictions.

In this chapter, I will propose argument classes and grammatical functions for inversion sentences which are consistent with the observations noted in Chapter 2 and I will comment on case marking and agreement in inversion sentences. I begin by reviewing the characteristics of the experiencer inversion construction.

The experiencer inversion construction revolves around two nominals one of which has nominative case and agrees with the verb while the other is non-nominative and does not trigger verb agreement. Either of the two nominals can be clause initial. In Chapter 2, I showed that clause-initial non-nominative NPs are not simply topicalized.

(199) a.   Deze boeken$_{nom.\ pl.}$ bevallen hem$_{dat.\ sg.}$.
           these books   please   him
           "These books please him./He enjoys these books."
      b.   Hem$_{dat.\ sg.}$ bevallen deze boeken.
           him   please   these books
           "These books please him./He enjoys these books."

The four subsections which follow this one discuss the grammatical functions of the two nominals in experiencer inversion sentences. In subsections 5.2.2 and 5.2.3 I will show that the nominative NP is a SUBJ in uninverted sentences and an OBJ in inverted sentences. Similarly, in subsections 5.2.4 and 5.2.5 I will suggest that the non-nominative NP is a SUBJ in inverted sentences and an OBJ in uninverted sentences.[46] Based on this, the simplest conclusion about ACs is that both nominals are in the general unrestricted class because this is the only argument class whose members can take on either the SUBJ or the OBJ function.[47] Therefore, I propose ((200) a) and ((200) b) as lexical forms for ((199) a) and ((199) b). In these lexical forms, *experiencer* is the thematic role of the non-nominative NP and *stimulus* is the role of the nominative NP.

(200) a.   'bevallen< experiencer   stimulus >'
                    SUBJ   OBJ

      b.   'bevallen< experiencer   stimulus >'
                    OBJ   SUBJ

I claim that there is no experiencer inversion rule which explicitly changes grammatical relations or argument classes or introduces a special value for the SUBJ function. The relation change follows simply from the fact that both arguments are general unrestricted and can take either the SUBJ or the OBJ function.

---

[46] This treatment of the non-nominative NP is based on a suggestion from Annie Zaenen.

[47] Another possibility is that the non-nominative NP is semantically restricted in which case the analysis of Dutch experiencer inversion would be similar to the analysis of English oblique inversion in the previous chapter.

In light of the grammatical function assignments in ((200) a) and ((200) b) there are two facts about case marking and agreement in experiencer inversion sentences which require some explanation. First, the nominative NP continues to agree with the verb even when it is an OBJ in inverted sentences. And, second, the non-nominative NP remains non-nominative even when it is a SUBJ.

In answer to the first question, I suggest that person and number agreement with verbs is based on case — nominative case particular — and not on grammatical functions. Agreement in LFG is handled by functional equations added to the lexical entries of verbs. I will not formulate any agreement equations here, but I will assume that verbs agree with a nominative argument and not necessarily with a SUBJ.[48]

With respect to the second question, I suggest that the non-nominative NPs carry quirky case marking. That is, they take an oblique case in spite of the fact that that they do not have an oblique function. I assume that the non-nominative NPs in inversion sentences carry the OBL_{goal} case.

Quirky case is characterized in some languages, such as Icelandic, by the *case preservation effect*. This term describes a situation where an NP keeps its case marking no matter what function it takes on. For example, in Icelandic, the dative object of *hjálpa* (help) keeps its dative case when it is the SUBJ of a passive ((201) b), when it is a non-thematic object of a higher clause ((201) c), and when it is a non-thematic subject in a higher clause ((201) d).[49] I claim that the case preservation effect is responsible for retention of non-nominative case in Dutch inverted sentences.

(201)a.   Ég hjálpa honum(DAT).
"I help him."
     b.   Honum(DAT) er hjálpað.
"He is helped."
     c.   Ég tel honum(DAT) hafa verið hjálpað.
"I believe him to have been helped."
     d.   Honum(DAT) er talið hafa verið hjálpað.
"He is believed to have been helped."

---

[48]This is consistent with an account of agreement developed by Bresnan, Maling, Thráinsson, and Zaenen in a workshop at Xerox PARC in June of 1984.

[49]Some languages seem to have quirky case marking but not case preservation. For example, in Japanese goal arguments of double object verbs have dative (ni) case in active sentences. However, they can appear with nominative case marking as subjects of passive sentences. The fact that they become subjects of passives shows that ni-marked NPs are actually not oblique. So, they must be quirky case marked OBJs which do not exhibit case preservation.

Following suggestions made at a workshop on Icelandic case marking[50], I assume that all cases are assigned in the lexicon. That is, all equations which assign case are attached to lexical forms of verbs rather than to positions in c-structure. Quirky case equations like ($\uparrow$ OBJ CASE) = OBL_{goal} or ($\uparrow$ SUBJ CASE) = OBL_{goal} override the default rules that assign nominative and accusative case to SUBJ and OBJ. Special rules also introduce the equation ($\uparrow$ OBJ CASE) = NOM when there is no nominative subject. ((202) a) and ((202) b) show more complete lexical entries for inflected forms of *bevallen* (like/please) with equations for case marking and agreement.

(202)a.   'bevallen< experiencer   stimulus >'
                      SUBJ   OBJ

        ($\uparrow$ TENSE) = PRESENT
        ($\uparrow$ SUBJ CASE) $=_c$ OBL_{goal}
        ($\uparrow$ OBJ CASE) $=_c$ NOM
        ($\uparrow$ OBJ NUM) $=_c$ PLURAL

    b.   'bevallen< experiencer   stimulus >'
                      OBJ   SUBJ

        ($\uparrow$ TENSE) = PRESENT
        ($\uparrow$ OBJ CASE) $=_c$ OBL_{goal}
        ($\uparrow$ SUBJ CASE) $=_c$ NOM
        ($\uparrow$ SUBJ NUM) $=_c$ PLURAL

The simplest account of case preservation associates the quirky case with an argument position[51] instead of with a grammatical function so that the argument will keep its case no matter what function it takes. Supporting this analysis, Andrews (1982) points out that it correctly predicts that verbs with non-thematic objects cannot impose a quirky case on those objects. I will not formulate a mechanism for case preservation here but I will assume that experiencer inversion verbs take the thematic roles of SUBJ and OBJ into account in order to appropriately assign the equations ($\uparrow$ OBJ CASE) = OBL_{goal} and ($\uparrow$ SUBJ CASE) = OBL_{goal}.[52]

The next four subsections closely examine the GFs of the nominative and non-nominative NPs in Dutch experiencer inversion sentences and provide evidence for the

---

[50] Center for the Study of Language and Information, Stanford Unviersity, June 1984

[51] See Levin (1981) and Levin & Simpson (1981).

[52] Andrews (1982) specifies a mechanism for case preservation in LFG, but it is not appropriate for the theory of AC.

grammatical function assignments in ((200) a) and ((200) b). Subsection 5.2.2 covers the least controversial of the GF assignments — the subjecthood of the nominative NP in uninverted sentences.

5.2.2. Subjecthood of the Nominative NP

In this subsection, I use control and coordination as tests for subjecthood. I show that the nominative NPs in uninverted sentences are subjects by showing that they can be controlled and that they can serve as the shared subjects of conjoined verb phrases.

In Chapter 4, I showed that being controllable is a good test for subjecthood in LFG because the analysis of control makes correct predictions about mixed subjecthood behavior of certain phrases. In particular, it predicts that some subjects could fail controllability tests for subjecthood because of their case marking and therefore explains the apparently paradoxical fact that these phrases pass some tests for subjecthood and not others. The discussion in Chapter 4 was based on three control constructions: anaphoric control of adjunct clauses and clausal subjects, functional control by non-thematic subjects and objects, and functional control by thematic subjects and objects. In this chapter, I use the same constructions as tests for subjecthood in Dutch. We can conclude that something is a subject if it can be controlled in one of these constructions. The three constructions are illustrated in ((203) a)-((203) c).

(203)a. Om nu naar huis te gaan is onaardig.
"To go home now is not nice." *anaphoric control*

b. Zij verlangen naar huis te gaan.
"They want to go home." *functional control by a matrix argument*

c. Zij schijnen dit leuk te vinden.
"They seem to think this is agreeable." *functional control by a non-thematic element*

As expected, the nominative NPs in uninverted sentences pass all control tests for subjecthood. This is illustrated here with the inversion verb *behagen* (please).

(204)a. Die ouders te behagen is onmogelijk.
"To please these parents is impossible." *anaphoric control*

b. De kinderen hopen hun ouders te behagen.
"The children hope to please their parents." *functional control by matrix argument*

c. De kinderen schijnen hun ouders te behagen.
"The children seem to please their parents." *functional control by a non-thematic element*

In this chapter, I will also use coordination as a test for subjecthood. This test is based on the ungrammaticality of sentences like ((205) c) and ((205) d). Presumably, ((205) a), which is grammatical, consists of two conjoined strings, *danced a jig* and *sang a ballad*, which share a subject, *Mary*. Similarly, ((205) b) consists of two conjoined phrases, *John likes* and *Bill hates*, which share a topicalized element, *Mary*. Sentences ((205) c) and ((205) d), however, are attempts to have two conjoined phrases, *is smart* and *John likes*, share an NP which serves as the subject of one and the topic of the other. From this data, we can draw the generalization that if conjoined strings share any phrases outside of the coordinate structure, those phrases must fill the same function in each conjunct.[53] The treatment of coordination introduced in Bresnan, Kaplan, and Peterson (in progress) enforces this generalization.[54]

(205) a.   Mary danced a jig and sang a ballad.
    b.   Mary, John likes and Bill hates.
    c.   * Mary is smart and John likes.
    d.   * Mary, John likes and is smart

The following sentences show that the same generalization holds in Dutch.

(206) a.   Maria at een koekje en zong een lied.
        "Maria ate a cookie and sang a ballad."
    b.   Dit schilderij bewonder ik en vindt Peter lelijk.
        "This painting, I admire and Peter finds ugly."
    c.   * Het schilderij is mooi en vindt Peter lelijk.
        "The painting is nice and Peter finds ugly."
    d.   * Het schilderij vindt Peter lelijk en is mooi.[55]
        "The painting, Peter finds ugly and is nice."

---

[53] Sentences ((205) c) and ((205) d) consist of a VP *is smart* conjoined with an S *John likes*. However, this cannot be the reason for the ungrammaticality because there are other instances where phrases of different categories may be conjoined. For example: *The children are happy and eating their dinner. He was acting really crazy and out of his mind.* Examples like these are discussed in Peterson (1982) and in Bresnan, Kaplan, and Peterson (in progress).

[54] In theory, there should be grammatical interpretations of ((205) c) and ((205) d) where *Mary* serves as the topic of both conjuncts. This problem is addressed by Falk (1982) who concludes, following Gazdar (1981), that subjects are not topicalized in the same way as non-subjects and that sentences with topicalized subjects cannot be conjoined with sentences having topicalized non-subjects. According to Falk's LFG account, sentences with topicalized subjects have different equations associated with them from sentences with other topicalized elements. This difference in equations, Falk claims, constitutes a difference in category. That is, an S with a topicalized subject is a different category from an S with a topicalized non-subject. Under this analysis, the reason for the ungrammaticality of ((205) c) and ((205) d) is that phrases of different categories have been conjoined.

However, Falk's account of this data conflicts with the Bresnan, Kaplan, and Peterson account of coordination which specifically allows phrases of different categories to be conjoined. So, there is more work to do on this problem.

[55] Note however, that when the topicalized element is stressed, sentences like ((206) d) may be grammatical: *DAT schilderij vindt Peter lelijk maar is mooi.* (THAT painting Peter finds ugly but is nice). ((206) c), on the other hand, cannot be salvaged in this way: **DAT schilderij is mooi maar vindt Peter lelijk.* (THAT painting is nice but Peter finds ugly.) Thanks to Yolande Post for pointing this out.

Coordination is used as a test for subjecthood in the following way: in order to test whether an NP is a SUBJ, find what might be the corresponding VP and conjoin it with something that is unquestionably a VP. If the sentence is grammatical, the NP that is shared by the conjuncts is probably the SUBJ of both and if the sentence is ungrammatical, the reason may be that the shared NP is not a SUBJ in one of the conjuncts.

The nominative NPs in uninverted sentences pass the coordination test for subjecthood. In sentences ((207) a) and ((207) b), *de kinderen* is unquestionably the SUBJ of *zijn knap* and therefore must also be the SUBJ of the other conjunct *bevallen hun ouders*.

(207)a.   De kinderen$_{stimulus}$ bevallen hun ouders$_{experiencer}$ en zijn knap.
"The children please their parents and are intelligent."
b.   De kinderen zijn knap en bevallen hun ouders$_{experiencer}$.
"The children are smart and please their parents."

5.2.3. Objecthood of the Nominative NP

The distribution of fronted *wat voor* phrases, discussed in den Besten (1982), shows that nominative NPs are OBJs of inverted sentences.

Corresponding to ((208) a) which has the fronted wh-phrase *wat voor boeken* (what kind of books), there is ((208) b) where only the wh-word *wat* has been fronted and the rest of the phrase *voor boeken* has been left in place. In ((209) a), the entire subject *wat voor mensen* of the embedded clause has been extracted. But in ((209) b) only *wat* has been fronted and the rest of the phrase remains in subject position of the embedded clause. Den Besten concludes that it is not possible to split *wat* from a wh-phrase when the phrase is a subject and that *wat* can be separated from the rest of the NP only when the NP is a direct object. (It is presumably irrelevant that ((208) b) involves extraction from a main clause while ((209) b) involves extraction from an embedded clause.)

(208)a.   Wat voor boeken heb jij deze week gelezen?
What kind of books have you this week read?
b.   Wat heb jij deze week voor boeken gelezen?
What have you this week kind of books read?
(209)a.   Wat voor mensen denk je dat daar leven?
What kind of people think you that live there?
b.   * Wat denk je dat voor mensen daar leven?
What think you that kind of people live there?

Wat climbs off of the nominative NP of experiencer inversion verbs when the word order is inverted — dative preceding nominative — as in ((210) b). *Wat* does not climb off of the nominative NP when the word order is non-inverted as in ((210) c).

(210) a. Wat voor dingen overkomen hem?
what for things happen him
"What kind of things happen to him?"
b. Wat overkomen hem voor dingen?
what happen him for things
"What kind of things happen to him?"
c. * Wat overkomen voor dingen hem?
what happen for things him
"What kind of things happen to him?"

If it is true that only direct objects launch *wat*, then ((210) b) is evidence that, in inverted word order, the nominative NP of experiencer inversion verbs is an OBJ. The same NP cannot launch *wat* when the word order is not inverted because, in that situation, the nominative NP is a SUBJ.

5.2.4. Subjecthood of the Non-Nominative NP

In this subsection, I apply tests for subjecthood to fronted non-nominative NPs in inverted sentences. I will show that these NPs fail several tests for subjecthood. However, as was the case for fronted PPs in English, failing these tests does not prove that the phrases in question are not subjects. On the contrary, the analyses of control and coordination in LFG actually predict that non-nominative subjects should fail certain tests for subjecthood even though they pass others. Assuming that the fronted non-nominative NPs are quirky case marked subjects, I will show that LFG makes the correct predictions about which subjecthood tests they will pass and which they will fail.

The LFG analyses of control and coordination make the following predictions about the behavior of non-nominative subjects. The first three of these were described in more detail in Chapter 4.

1. It should not be possible to anaphorically control a non-nominative subject because anaphorically controlled elements are introduced as PRO in the lexical entries of their governing verbs. PRO does not have the appropriate case features to satisfy the quirky case requirements of certain verbs.

2. It should not be possible for a thematic argument of a higher clause to functionally control a non-nominative NP in a lower clause because the controller and the controllee have conflicting case requirements. Furthermore, if obliques are not "flat", they will not satisfy the semantic requirements of the matrix verb because they will not have a PRED feature at the top level.

3. It should be possible for a non-thematic NP in a higher clause to functionally control a non-nominative NP in a lower clause. Since verbs do not impose

semantic restrictions on non-thematic functions that they govern, it will not matter that the oblique phrase lacks a PRED feature at the top level. Furthermore, in the theory of case proposed at the CSLI workshop on Icelandic case marking, although all cases are assigned lexically, assignments of case to non-arguments are optional. Therefore, a non-thematic controller and a non-nominative controllee will not have conflicting case requirements.

4. It should not be possible to conjoin a VP that takes a nominative subject with a VP that takes a non-nominative subject because the two VPs will impose conflicting case requirements on the subject that they share.[56]

The following examples show that fronted experiencers cannot be anaphorically controlled or functionally controlled by thematic arguments of a matrix verb.

(211)a.   * Boeken bevallen is geweldig.
      books to please is fantastic
      "To like books is fantastic"
b.   * Ik/me hoop(t) deze boeken te bevallen.
      I/me hope(s) these books to please
      "I hope to like these books"

The situation is far less clear for control by non-thematic elements. ((212) a) *could* involve control by a non-thematic SUBJ in the matrix clause. But it could also be an instance of topicalization. Because Dutch is a verb-second language, ((212) a) could be the result of topicalizing ((212) b). However, the fact that the fronted experiencer inverts with the tensed verb in ((213) b) indicates that it is not a topicalized element, and is, in fact, a SUBJ in the matrix clause.

(212)a.   Hem schijnen deze boeken te bevallen.
      (to) him seem these books to please.
      "These books seem to please him"
b.   Deze boeken schijnen hem te bevallen.
      "These books seem to please him"
(213)a.   Schijnen deze boeken hem te bevallen?
      "Do these books seem to please him?"
b.   Schijnen hem deze boeken te bevallen?
      "Do these books seem to please him?"

The next set of sentences show that it is not possible to conjoin the strings *de appels bevallen* (like the apples) and *knap zijn* (are intelligent), the problem being that the conjoined phrases must share a SUBJ, but they impose different case requirements on it. *De appels*

---

[56] In conflict with these predictions, Icelandic quirky case marked subjects can (marginally) be anaphorically controlled (Andrews 1982) and Icelandic verb phrases requiring nominative subjects can be conjoined with Icelandic verb phrases requiring non-nominative subjects.

bevallen requires a non-nominative SUBJ while *knap zijn* requires a nominative SUBJ, so the SUBJ of the conjoined VPs will always fail to meet the requirements of one of the conjuncts.

(214) a. * De kinderen$_{experiencer}$ bevallen de appels$_{NOM}$ en zijn knap.
 The children please the apples and are intelligent
 "The children like the apples and are intelligent."
 b. * Mij$_{experiencer}$ heeft het$_{NOM}$ veel geld gekost en ben teleurgesteld.
 Me has it a lot of money cost and am disappointed.
 "It cost me a lot of money and I'm disappointed."
 c. * Ik ben teleurgesteld en heeft het veel geld gekost.
 I am disappointed and has it a lot of money cost.
 "I am disappointed and it cost me a lot of money."

Of course, it is possible to conjoin phrases like *ligt dat werk niet* (not like that work) and *lukt het niet* (not succeed in it) because they both require non-nominative subjects.[57] Notice that the sentence below has a second interpretation where two full sentences have been conjoined which do not share a subject.

(215) Mij ligt dat werk niet en lukt het niet.
 Me lies that work not and succeeds it not
 "I do not like the work and it does not go well for me."
 "I do not like the work and it does not go well in general."

In conclusion, fronted non-nominative NPs pass one test for subjecthood and fail three. However, we can still conclude that they are subjects because the LFG analyses of control and coordination actually predict that non-nominative subjects should pattern in this way.

5.2.5. Objecthood of Non-Nominative NPs

The only diagnostic for OBJs that I know of in Dutch is the *wat voor* test described in Subection 5.2.3. Non-initial non-nominative NPs fail this test. In ((216) b), the word order is inverted and the experiencer, therefore, follows the nominative stimulus argument. In this sentence, only the word *wat* has been fronted while the rest of the phrase remains in object position at the end of the sentence.

(216) a. Wat voor mensen bevallen die dingen.
 "What kind of people like those things."
 b. * Wat bevallen die dingen voor mensen.

I do not have an analysis of the *wat voor* construction, but I suspect that it is similar to

---

[57] One of my informants does not accept this sentence.

Quantifier Float which, in many languages, does not apply to oblique NPs.[58] Therefore, I suggest that non-nominative NPs fail the test because they have oblique case marking, not because they are not OBJs.

5.2.6. Conclusion

Non-nominative subjects pose an interesting problem for linguistic theory because they pass some tests for subjecthood and fail others. One way to deal with this is to throw out the notion of subject as a unique grammatical relation and talk instead about more and less subject-like things. (See, for example Comrie (1981).) Another solution to the dilemna, embodied in Perlmutter's notion of Working 1, is the idea that some non-nominative NPs are subjects at some levels of representation but not at others. If this were true then the mixed behavior of non-nominative subjects would follow from applying the subjecthood tests at different levels of representation. Perlmutter (1982), for example claims that some rules are sensitive to the presence of final 1's while others are sensitive to the presence of Working 1's. Working 1's are NPs that are 1's in the initial stratum and terms (1, 2, or 3) in the final stratum. In this chapter and in Chapter 4, I take a different approach to non-nominative subjects, claiming that they are, in fact, subjects but that some of the subjecthood tests are sabotaged by their case marking.

This treatment of non-nominative subjects has a considerable amount of explanatory value. First, it is based on a principled, restricted view of what counts as a test for subjecthood. In order to talk about this, I propose a distinction between observation-based tests and prediction-based tests. Observation-based tests are formed from an observation about the behavior of NPs that are unquestionably subjects. For example, we might observe that subjects are nominative and trigger verb agreement. Prediction-based tests are actual predictions that the theory makes about the behavior of subjects. For example, the theory of coordination tells us that if two VPs are conjoined then the NP that they are predicated of must be the SUBJ of each. In my analysis, I used only prediction-based tests for subjecthood. I reject observation-based tests such as case marking and agreement because nothing in the theory connects them in any way with subjecthood. Rejecting observation-based tests considerably softens the problem of mixed subjecthood behavior by reducing the amount of conflicting data.

---

[58]For example, Watanabe (1985) shows that Quantifier Float in Japanese is sensitive to case marking rather than grammatical relations. Quantifier Float in Japanese applies to nominative (ga) and accusative (o) NPs, but it does not apply to dative (ni) NPs.

Second, the LFG analyses of control and coordination actually predict that non-nominative subjects should fail certain prediction-based tests for subjecthood because of their case marking. So, the mixed subjecthood behavior of non-nominative NPs follows from already existing parts of the theory. It is not necessary to bend the theory in any way to accomodate this behavior. A consequence of this is that the notion of Working 1, which as far as I can tell was introduced only to handle the apparently paradoxical behavior of non-nominative NPs, is unnecessary.[59]

Third, I believe that it is significant that dummy subjects exhibit almost exactly the same kind of mixed subjecthood behavior as non-nominative subjects (at least in English). They can be functionally controlled by non-thematic elements but they cannot be anaphorically controlled or functionally controlled by matrix arguments. Furthermore, a string requiring a dummy SUBJ cannot be conjoined with a string requiring a non-dummy SUBJ.

(217) a. There seem to be people here.
 b. * To be people here would be nice.
  (Cannot mean *For there to be people here would be nice.*)
 c. * There tried to be people here.

My approach to non-nominatives provides a unified account of the mixed subjecthood behavior of dummies and non-nominative subjects. Everything is predicted by the theories of control and coordination.

My treatment of the inversion construction in Dutch is very simple yet seems to cover all the relevant data. The unaccusative behavior of inversion verbs and the optionality of inversion in Dutch both follow from the proposal that inversion verbs have two general unrestricted arguments and no subjective unrestricted argument.

5.3. Auxiliary selection and Rule Mismatches

In Chapter 2, I showed that auxiliary selection is a UR by showing that it distinguishes between active transitive verbs and passive verbs and that it splits the intransitive verbs into two groups: those that, like the passive verbs, take *zijn* and those that, like the active transitive verbs, take *hebben*. This section addresses a particular problem that arises when auxiliary selection is compared to passivization and experiencer inversion which are also URs. All of

---

[59]Watanabe (1984) shows that the notion of Working 1 is not only unnecessary but also does not work in Japanese. She also claims that the mixed behavior of non-nominative NPs should be attributed to their case marking and not to any peculiarity in their grammatical function.

these rules supposedly separate the set of unaccusative verbs from the set of unergative verbs. And, furthermore, they separate the two classes of verbs on syntactic grounds depending on whether they have a subjective unrestricted argument. However, it turns out that there are verbs which are treated as if they were unaccusative by some rules but are treated as if they were unergative by others. This type of discrepancy is unexpected in the theory of AC and, in fact, casts doubt on the reality of AC as a level of representation in Dutch. Nevertheless, I will present a possible resolution to these problems, which retains AC as a level of representation. The solution is based on adding additional semantic constraints to some of the URs.

Disagreements between URs as to whether a verb is unaccusative or unergative will be called *mismatches*.[60]

5.3.1. Description of Mismatches

The first type of mismatch to be discussed involves verbs which do not passivize but take *hebben* as the aspectual auxiliary. If not passivizing is characteristic of unaccusative verbs and taking *hebben* is characteristic of unergative verbs, then the following examples require some explanation.[61]

(218)a. Het concert heeft een hele tijd geduurd. (P 55)
         "The concert has lasted a long time."
    b.   * Er werd door het concert een hele tijd geduurd.
         "It was lasted a long time by the concert."
(219)a. Dat blok hout heeft goed gebrand. (P 66)
         "That block of wood has burned well."
    b.   * Er werd door dat blok hout goed gebrand.
         "It was burned well by that block of wood."
(220)a. Het heeft veel geld gekost.
         "It has cost a lot of money."
    b.   * Er is veel geld gekost.
         "It is cost a lot of money."
(221)a. De badkamer heeft gestonken.
         "The bathroom has stunk."
    b.   * Er wordt door de badkamer gestonken.
         "It is stunk by the bathroom."

Many stative verbs such as *kosten* (cost) and *duren* (last) pattern in this way as do verbs like *stinken* (stink) and *murmelen* (murmur) which describe emission of sensory stimulus from

---

[60] Mismatches are also discussed by Knecht & Levin (1984) and Knecht (in preparation).

[61] Annotations in the right margin refer to example numbers in Perlmutter (1978).

inanimate objects. The expected pattern of AUX-selection and impersonal passivization is exhibited by *blijven* (remain) which takes *zijn* and does not passivize, and by *transpireren* (perspire) which takes *hebben* and passivizes.

(222)a. De kinderen zijn in Amsterdam gebleven. (P 54a)
"The children are (i.e. have) remained in Amsterdam."
b. * Er werd door de kinderen in Amsterdam gebleven. (P 54b)
"It was remained in Amsterdam by the children."
(223)a. Ik heb getranspireerd.
"I have perspired."
b. Er wordt door de mensen getranspireerd.
"It was perspired by the people."

Another mismatch involves verbs that undergo experiencer inversion and take *hebben*. Again, if undergoing inversion is an indicator of unaccusativity and taking *hebben* is an indicator of unergativity, then the following examples are unexpected.

(224)a. Het zal jou berouwen dat...
Jou zal het berouwen dat...
"You will regret it that..."
b. Het heeft mij berouwed.
"I have regretted it."
(225)a. Deze jurk past mij niet.
Mij past deze jurk niet.
This dress does not fit me.
b. Deze jurk heeft mij niet gepast.
"This dress has not fit me."
(226)a. Dit toneelstuk spreekt mij aan.
Mij spreekt dit toneelstuk wel aan.
The play appeals to me.
b. Dit toneelstuk heeft mij aangesproken.
"The play has appealed to me."

The expected pattern is illustrated by *bevallen* (please) which takes *zijn* and undergoes experiencer inversion, and by *haten* (hate) which takes *hebben* and does not invert.

The converse type of mismatch also exists. There are verbs that act unaccusative with respect to AUX-selection but act unergative with respect to another rule. The following verbs take *zijn* and successfully undergo impersonal passivization. This is unexpected because verbs that take *zijn* are unaccusative and verbs that passivize are unergative. Verbs that pattern in this way include those that describe directed (not aimless) motion.

(227)a. I ben naar school gelopen.
"I am (i.e. have) walked to school."
b. Er wordt door de kinderen naar school gelopen.
"It was walked to school by the children."

(228)a. Ik ben opgestaan.
"I got up."
b. Er wordt door iedereen opgestaan.
"It is stood up by everybody."

It is interesting to note that not all possible mismatches between rules occur. For example, as expected, no experiencer inversion verb passivizes. Subsection 5.3.3 presents a solution to the mismatches which clarifies why the processes of AUX-selection, impersonal passivization, and experiencer inversion are compatible in some ways as indicators of unaccusativity and incompatible in others.

5.3.2. A Question about the Nature of Mismatches

Mismatches are a problem because they seem to require certain verbs to be simultaneously unaccusative and unergative. In terms of AC, this means that they require a verb to have a subjective unrestricted argument and at the same time not have a subjective unrestricted argument. An obvious way to resolve the mismatches is to do away with AC entirely and reformulate the URs totally in semantic terms. For example, suppose that auxiliary selection only took into account the semantic class of verbs that it applied to and suppose that it included directed manner of motion verbs in the set of verbs that take *zijn*. Then there would be no conflict between auxiliary selection and passivization. Directed manner of motion verbs would passivize by virtue of having arguments with the agent role and they would take *zijn* by virtue of their semantic class. This would not be a problem because nothing prevents a verb from having an agent and at the same time being a directed motion verb. Under this approach mismatches would be expected instead of being problematic.

Furthermore, something about the nature of URs makes it seem quite likely that they are defined semantically (in terms of thematic roles and semantic classes) rather than syntactically (in terms of AC). In my investigation of URs in English and Dutch, I found very few URs which distinguish all unaccusative verbs as a syntactic class from all unergative verbs as a syntactic class. Instead, many URs pick out a semantically defined subset of unaccusative verbs. In English, There-Insertion, Oblique-Inversion, Adjectival Passivization, and Resultative Secondary Predication all seem to be URs, but for each construction, it is easy to find a set of unaccusative verbs that do not fit. For example, STAY verbs do not undergo RSP. So, *He stayed bored* cannot mean that he stayed until he was bored and *He stood tired* cannot mean that he stood until he was tired. Similarly, change of state verbs do not undergo There-Insertion even though other URs treat them as if they were unaccusative. So, we have ungrammatical sentences like *There froze a lake* and *There thickened a sauce on the stove. In short, each English UR applies to a semantically restricted set of unaccusative verbs.

Now notice that the reason for having a level of representation is to set up distinctions that could only be handled clumsily at other levels of representation. For example, if we did not have a level of grammatical functions, we would have to refer to SUBJs by describing the positions they can occupy and the thematic roles they can have. (Simpson and Bresnan (1982) show that this is undesirable in Warlpiri.) It appears, though, that AC is not doing its job as a level of representation because it does not protect us from defining rules using messy disjunctions of thematic roles. Many of the thematic rules formulated in terms of the distinction between subjective unrestricted and general unrestricted arguments at AC need to have messy semantic restrictions put on them anyway and very few rules refer unconditionally to the set of subjective unrestricted or general unrestricted arguments. Therefore, it seems that AC could be eliminated as a level of representation, URs could be stated semantically, and mismatches would not be a problem.

However, there are some convincing reasons to keep AC as a level of representation. First, if AC were not available, all of the URs would have to separate unaccusative from unergative verbs on semantic/thematic grounds. But then the rules would seem to miss syntactic generalizations about the treatment of active transitive verbs and passive verbs. Second, AC neatly represents the difference between canonical and non-canonical subjects as described in Chapter 2. And, third, passivization is at least one rule in Dutch that does distinguish all unaccusative verbs from all unergative verbs. So, at least two generalizations — one about which verbs can passivize and one about which SUBJs can be OBJs in related sentences — do not mismatch and, because of their salience, I consider them to be justification for keeping AC as a level of representation.

5.3.3. A Syntactic Account of Auxiliary Selection and Mismatches

In this section, I propose a solution to the rule mismatches which is based on the assumption that auxiliary selection is governed by syntactic as well as semantic restrictions. The syntactic restriction, formulated in (229), states that verbs with canonical subjects cannot take *zijn* as the aspectual auxiliary.

(229)   **Condition on the use of *zijn*:**

        Use *zijn* with lexical forms which do not have subjective unrestricted arguments.

(229) captures syntactic generalizations about auxiliary selection. Active transitive verbs all have subjective unrestricted arguments (except for experiencer inversion verbs) and, therefore, take *hebben*. But passive verbs do not have subjective unrestricted arguments and, therefore, take *zijn*. Unaccusative verbs pattern with passive verbs because they too do not have subjective unrestricted arguments while unergative verbs pattern with the transitive verbs because they have subjective unrestricted arguments.

Taking (229) to be a syntactic elsewhere condition, I propose that there are some semantically defined exceptions which override it. For example, one class of exceptions is the set of verbs describing emission of sensory stimulus from inanimate objects. Since these verbs do not passivize, we conclude that they do not have a subjective unrestricted argument. However, in spite of this, they take *hebben*. Another class of exceptions includes some of the experiencer inversion verbs which also take *hebben* even though they do not passivize. And, finally, a major class of exceptions are the directed manner of motion verbs which take *zijn* even though passivization indicates that they have subjective unrestricted arguments.

The mechanism that I propose for auxiliary selection is to mark verbs in the lexicon with one of two equations: ($\uparrow$ AUX) = *zijn* or ($\uparrow$ AUX) = *hebben*. First, the exceptional classes of verbs are marked with the appropriate equations and then the syntactic elsewhere condition fills in the equations on the remaining verbs. In addition, the auxiliary verbs *hebben* and *zijn*, carry the equations ($\uparrow$ XCOMP AUX) $=_c$ *zijn* and ($\uparrow$ XCOMP AUX) $=_c$ *hebben* respectively in order to insure that they occur with the matching complement verbs.

((230) a) shows a partial lexical entry for *lopen* (walk). The lexical form will passivize because it has a subjective unrestricted argument, but it is marked with *zijn* because it is a verb of directed motion. Conversely, the lexical form for *stinken* (stink) in ((230) b) will not passivize because it has no subjective unrestricted argument, but takes *hebben* because it describes emission of sensory stimulus.

(230)a.   'lopen< $\underline{\text{agent}}$[62]   goal >'
                SUBJ   OBL$_{goal}$
      ($\uparrow$ AUX) $=_c$ *zijn*

b.   'stinken< theme >'
                SUBJ
      ($\uparrow$ AUX) $=_c$ *hebben*

---

[62] This argument should more accurately be labelled both agent and theme because it volitionally carries out the action, but it is also the argument that undergoes a change of location.

To summarize the discussion of rule mismatches: they appear at first to be inconsistent with the notion of argument classification and seem to indicate that URs are actually defined in semantic terms. However, URs typically separate all active transitive verbs from all passive verbs and it would be very difficult to do this semantically because an active verb and its corresponding passive are in the same semantic class and have the same thematic roles. Nevertheless, I have shown in this section that mismatches can be resolved by formulating URs in terms of AC along with semantic exceptions and constraints.

5.4. Conclusion

This thesis introduces a notion of argument classification into LFG and illustrates its use in the theory. AC allows the theory to represent four basic properties of relation changing rules: semantic conditioning, syntactic productivity, sensitivity to two types of subject, and apparent directionality when it comes to SUBJ/OBJ relation changes. Furthermore, using AC, it is possible to formulate a theory of possible relation changing rules. The constraints on possible rules are based on the distinction between semantically restricted and semantically unrestricted argument classes along with the distinction between semantically encoded and freely encoded grammatical functions. In addition to its general use in the theory of relation changing rules, AC provides insight into Burzio's Generalization, the treatment of double object verbs, and the treatment of non-nominative subjects. Rule mismatches, which appear at first to cast doubt on the theory of AC, turn out only to show that rules which are sensitive to argument classification tend to be semantically constrained.

Chapter 6
REFERENCES

AISSEN, J. (1975) "Presentational-there Insertion: A cyclic root transformation" in Robin E. Grossman, L. James San, and Timothy J. Vance (eds.) *Papers from the Eleventh Regional Meeting of the Chicago Linguistic Society*.

ANDERSON, S. (1977) "Comments on the Paper by Wasow", in A. Akmajian, P. Cullicover, and T. Wasow (eds.), *Formal Syntax*, Academic Press, pages 361-377.

ANDREWS, A.D. (1982) "The Representation of Case in Modern Icelandic", in Bresnan (ed.) chapter 7, pages 427-503.

BACH, E. (1980) "In Defense of Passive", *Linguistics and Philosophy*, Vol. 3, pages 297-341.

BAKER, M. (1983) "Objects, Themes, and Lexical Rules in Italian", in Levin, Rappaport, and Zaenen (eds.), pages 1-46.

BOWERS, J.S. (1976) "On Surface Structure Grammatical Relations and the Structure-Preserving Hypothesis", *Linguistic Analysis* Vol. 2 No. 3, pages 225-242.

BRESNAN, J. (ed.) (1982) *The Mental Representation of Grammatical Relations*, MIT Press: Cambridge.

BRESNAN, J. (1982a) "The Passive in Lexical Theory", in Bresnan (ed.), pages 3-86.

BRESNAN, J. (1982b) "Polyadicity", in Bresnan (ed.), pages 149-172.

BRESNAN, J. (1982c) "Control and Complementation", in Bresnan (ed.), pages 282-391.

BRESNAN, J., K. HALVORSEN, & J. MALING (in progress) "Invariants of Anaphoric Binding Systems".

BRESNAN, J., R. KAPLAN, & P. PETERSON (in progress) "Coordination and the Flow of Information Through Phrase Structure".

BURZIO, L. (1981) *Intransitive Verbs and Italian Auxiliaries*, Ph.D. Dissertation M.I.T.

CASSELLS (1978) Dutch Dictionary. Macmillan:NY.

CHOMSKY, N. (1981) *Lectures on Government and Binding*, Foris Publications.

COMRIE, B. (1976) *Aspect*, Cambrige University Press.

COMRIE, B. (1981) *Language Universals and Linguistic Typology*, University of Chicago Press: Chicago.

CRUSE, D.A. (1973) "Some Thoughts on Agentivity", *Journal of Linguistics*.

DEN BESTEN, H. (1982) "Some Remarks on the Ergative Hypothesis", in Groningen Arbeiten zur Germanistischen Linguistik, Vol. 21 pages 61-82.

DONALDSON, B. (1981) *Dutch Reference Grammar*, Martinus Nijhoff: The Hague.

DOWTY, D. (1979) *Word Meaning and Montague Grammar*, Reidel: Dordrecht.

EINARSSON, S. (1945) *Icelandic*, Johns Hopkins University Press, Baltimore.

EMONDS, J. (1976) *A Transformational Approach to English Syntax: Root, Structure-Preserving, and Local Transformations*, Ch 2. New York: Academic Press.

FALK, Y. (1982) "Subjects and Long Distance Dependencies", to appear in Linguistic Analysis.

FILLMORE, C. (1968) "The Case for Case", in E. Bach and R.T. Harms, eds., *Universals In Linguistic Theory*, Holt, Rinehart, and Winston: New York.

FRIÐJÓNSSON, J. (1978) *A Course in Modern Icelandic*, Utgefandi: Timartid Skak, Reykjavik.

FREIDIN, R. and L. BABBY (1982) "On the Interaction of Lexical and Structural Properties: Case Structure in Russian", ms. Cornell University.

GAZDAR, G. (1981) "Unbounded Dependencies and Coordinate Structure", *Linguistic Inquiry* 12.2, pages 155-184.

GRANGER-LEGRAND, S. (1983) *The be + Past Participle Construction in Spoken English*, North-Holland: NY.

GRIMSHAW, J. (1979) "The Structure-Preserving Constraint: A review of *A Transformational Approach to English Syntax* by J.E. Emonds", *Linguistic Analysis*, Vol. 5 Num. 3, pages 313-343.

GRIMSHAW J. (1982a) "On the Nature of Romance Reflexive Clitics" in Bresnan (ed.) chapter 2, pages 87-148.

GRIMSHAW J. (1982b) "Subcategorization and Grammatical Relations", in A. Zaenen, (ed.).

GRUBER, J. S. (1976) *Lexical Structures in Syntax and Semantics*, North Holland Publishing Company: Amsterdam.

GUERSSEL, M., K. HALE, M. LAUGHREN, B. LEVIN, & J. WHITE EAGLE (1985) "A Cross-Linguistic Study of Transitivity Alternations", CLS 21.

HALE, K. & M. LAUGHREN (1983) "The Structure of Verbal Entries", ms. MIT.

HALLE, M., J. BRESNAN & G. MILLER, eds. (1978) *Linguistic Theory and Psychological Reality*, MIT Press: Cambridge.

HALLIDAY, M.A.K. (1967) "Notes on Transitivity and Theme in English: part I", *Journal of Linguistics*, vol 3.

HARRIS, A. "On the Loss of a Rule of Syntax" in *Current Issues in Linguistic Theory* Vol. 14 pps. 165-171, *Amsterdam Studies in the Theory and History of Linguistic Science IV, Papers from the Fourth International Conference on Historical Linguistics*, Traugott, E.C. et. al. eds.

HERMON, G. (1981) *Non-nominative Subject Constructions in the Government and Binding Framework*, Ph.D. Dissertation, University of Illinois.

HOEKSTRA, T. (1984) *Transitivity: Grammatical Relations in Government and Binding Theory*, Foris: Dordrecht.

JACKENDOFF, R. (1976) "Toward an Explanatory Semantic Representation", Linguistic Inquiry 7.1, pages 89-150.

JACKENDOFF, R. (1978) "Grammar as Evidence for Conceptual Structure", in Halle, Bresnan, and Miller eds., pages 201-228.

JACKENDOFF (1984) *Semantics and Cognition*, M.I.T. Press: Cambridge.

KAPLAN, R. and J. BRESNAN (1982) "Lexical Functional Grammar: a Formal System for Grammatical Representation", in Bresnan (ed). chapter 4, pages 173-281.

KEYSER, S.J. & T. ROEPER (1984) "On the Middle and Ergative Constructions in English", Linguistic Inquiry Vol. 15 no. 3, pages 381-416.

KNECHT, L. (in preparation) *Subject and Object in Turkish*, Ph.D. Dissertation, M.I.T.

KNECHT & LEVIN (1984) "Unaccusative Mismatches", Paper Presented at the Symposium on Grammatical Relations, SUNY Buffalo.

LANGENDOEN, D.T. (1973) "The Problem of Grammatical Relations in Surface Structure", in Kurt Jankowsky, (ed.) *Georgetown University Round Table on Languages and Linguistics*.

LEVIN, B. (1983) *On the Nature of Ergativity*, Ph.D. Dissertation, MIT.

LEVIN, B. & M. RAPPAPORT (1985) "The Formation of Adjectival Passives", Lexicon Project Working Papers #2, M.I.T.

LEVIN, L. (1981) "Lexical Representations of Quirky Case in Icelandic", ms. MIT.

LEVIN, L. and J. SIMPSON (1981) "Quirky Case and the Structure of Icelandic Lexical Entries", CLS 17, Roberta Hendrick, Carrie Masek, and Mary Frances Miller (eds.)

LEVIN, L., M. RAPPAPORT, & A. ZAENEN (eds.) (1983) *Papers in Lexical Functional Grammar*, IULC.

MARANTZ, A. (1984) *On the Nature of Grammatical Relations*, MIT Press:Cambridge, MA.

MASSAM, D. (1984) "On the Derivability of Burzio's Generalization", Presented at the Annual Meeting of the Linguistic Society of America.

MOHANAN, K.P. (1982) "Grammatical Relations and Clause Structure in Malayalam", in Bresnan, ed., pages 504-589.

MOHANAN, K.P. (1983) "Functional and Anaphoric Control", *Linguistic Inquiry* 14.4.

NEIDLE, C. (1982) "Case Agreement in Russian" in Bresnan (ed.) pages 391-426.

NEIDLE, C. (1982) *The Role of Case in Russian Syntax*, Ph.D. Dissertation, MIT.

PERLMUTTER, D. (1978) "Impersonal Passives and the Unaccusative Hypothesis", *Proceedings of the Fourth Annual Meeting of the Berkeley Linguistics Society*.

PERLMUTTER, D. (1979) "Working 1's and Inversion in Italian, Japanese, and Quechua", *Proceedings of the Berkeley Linguistic Society*, pages 277-324.

PERLMUTTER, D. (1982) "Syntactic Representation, Syntactic Levels, and the Notion of Subject", in P. Jacobson and G. Pullum, eds., *The Nature of Syntactic Representation*, Reidel: Dordrecht.

PERLMUTTER, D. (ed.) (1983) *Studies in Relational Grammar 1*, University of Chicago Press: Chicago.

PERLMUTTER, D. & C. ROSEN (eds.) (1984) *Studies in Relational Grammar 2*, University of Chicago Press: Chicago.

PERLMUTTER, D. and P. POSTAL (1983a) "Toward a Universal Characterization of Passivization", in D. Perlmutter, (ed).

PERLMUTTER & POSTAL (1983b) "Some Proposed Laws of Basic Clause Structure", in D. Perlmutter, (ed).

PERLMUTTER, D. & P. POSTAL (1984) "The 1-Advancement Exclusiveness Law", in Perlmutter and Rosen, (eds).

PETERSON, P. (1982) "Conjunction in LFG", ms. University of Newcastle.

RANDALL, J. (1983) "A Lexical Approach to Causatives", Journal of Linguistic Research, 2.3.

RAPPAPORT, M. (1983) "On the Nature of Derived Nominals", in Levin, Rappaport, and Zaenen (eds), pages 113-142.

ROSEN, C. (1981) *The Relational Structure of Reflexive Clauses: Evidence from Italian*, Ph.D. Dissertation, Harvard.

ROSEN, C. (1984) "The Interface between Semantic Roles and Initial Grammatical Relations", in Perlmutter and Rosen (eds).

ROSS, J.R. (1974a) "There, There, (There, (There, (There...)))", in CLS 10, Michael La Galy, Robert Fox, and Anthony Bruck (eds).

ROTHSTEIN (1983) *The Syntactic Forms of Predication*, Ph.D. Dissertation, M.I.T.

ROGNVALDSON, E. (1982) "We Need (Some Kind of a) Rule of Conjuction Reduction", Linguistic Inquiry 13.3, pages 557-561.

SAFIR, K. (1982) *Syntactic Chains and the Definiteness Effect*, Ph.D. Dissertation, M.I.T.

SIMPSON, J. (1983a) "Resultatives", in Levin, Rappaport, and Zaenen (eds), pages 143-158.

SIMPSON, J. (1983b) *Aspects of Warlpiri Morphology and Syntax*, PhD thesis, MIT.

SIMPSON, J. & J. BRESNAN (1982) "Control and Obviation in Warlpiri", Proceedings of the First Annual West Coast Conference on Formal Linguistics.

THRÁINSSON, H. (1979) *On Complementation in Icelandic*, NY:Garland.

VENDLER, Z. (1967) *Linguistics in Philosophy*, Cornell University Press.

WASOW, T. (1977) "Transformations and the Lexicon" in *Formal Syntax*, pages 327-360.

WASOW, T. (1980) "Major and Minor Rules in Lexical Grammar" in Teun Hoekstra, Harry van der Hulst, and Michael Moorgat (eds.) *Lexical Grammar*, Dordrecht: Foris Publications.

WASOW, T., I.A. SAG, & G. NUNBERG, "Idioms: an Interim Report", in Shiro Hattori and Kazuko Inoue (eds.) *Proceedings of the XIIIth International Congress of Linguistics*. CIPL: Tokyo, pages 102-115.

WILLIAMS, E. (1984) "*There*-Insertion", Linguistic Inquiry, Vol. 15 No. 1, pages 131-154.

WATANABE, T. (1985) *The Inversion Construction in Japanese*, Masters Thesis, University of Pittsburgh.

ZAENEN, A. (ed.) (1982) *Subject and Other Subjects*, IULC.

ZAENEN, A. and J. MALING (1983) "Passive and Oblique Case", in Levin, Rappaport, and Zaenen (eds), pages 159-191.